YOUR
BEST
INTEREST

TOM WEISHAAR

YOUR BEST INTEREST

A Money Book for the Computer Age

**Includes Spreadsheet Formulas
For Personal Computer Users**

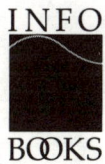
INFO BOOKS

© 1985 by Tom Weishaar
Published by InfoBooks, Santa Monica, CA 90406

All rights reserved. No part of this book
may be reproduced, in any form or by any means,
without permission in writing from the publisher.

Cover design: Gloria Garland
Text design: Marvin Warshaw

Published in the United States of America

10 9 8 7 6 5 4 3 2 1

ISBN 0-931137-00-4

P.O. Box 1018
Santa Monica, CA 90406

ABOUT THIS BOOK

You buy a home and get a $50,000, 30-year mortgage. At a 12 per cent interest rate your monthly payment would be $563.85. Multiply that monthly payment times 12 and times 30 years and it becomes clear that you'll actually pay back $202,986.00! Did you realize you'd spend more than $150,000 to borrow $50,000 for 30 years?

One lender offers you a $50,000, 30-year home mortgage at 14 per cent interest. A second lender offers the same amount at 13.75 per cent, but charges a 3 per cent origination fee. Which is the better deal?

Unless you have a masters in business administration, you probably made it through your entire formal education without so much as an introduction to what's known as the *time value of money*.

Yet, as life proceeds, you're probably finding yourself involved in time-sensitive financial transactions more and more often. When you borrow money for a car or home, when you invest in an IRA, a pension fund, or life insurance—even when you open a checking account or use a credit card, you are making financial decisions that can have a profound effect on your prosperity.

Most of us—with the exception of the bankers, brokers, and corporate finance officers among us—have no idea how powerful the time value of money is. We have no idea how to compare investment or loan alternatives. Salespeople lure us with what appear to be favorable terms and, too often, we take the bait.

This book is a light and enlightening work designed to demystify money. What you missed in your formal education you can pick up here informally. The concepts are not difficult. Anyone who made it through high school algebra can easily grasp what we'll be doing here.

Understanding the time value of money is of little use unless you can also calculate it for various situations. These calculations are difficult to do with pencil and paper—which is why this subject area isn't often taught in schools. However, today's personal computers can calculate and recalculate and recalculate time value as fast as you can enter the numbers.

This book consists of two major parts. Part I, which includes the first four chapters, will show you how to do these interest-rate calculations. Each of these chapters is further divided into two main sections.

The first section provides essential background material—the concepts underlying, and the words associated with, interest-related transactions.

The second section provides a tutorial that demonstrates how to do actual calculations. You will learn how to solve interest-rate problems in a step-by-step procedure. Since we'll use your computer to calculate solutions, you will be able to concentrate on the implications of the financial transactions themselves and let the computer handle all the arithmetic.

The instructions provided in the tutorials include all the information you need to calculate interest rates using a spreadsheet program (such as VisiCalc, Multiplan, or Lotus 1-2-3). The instructions assume you already know how to use your spreadsheet. However, you don't have to be an expert user. Herein you'll find complete templates for solving interest-rate problems that use just the simplest spreadsheet commands and functions.

In addition, each tutorial includes sample situations, with answers; you can use these to further expand your understanding of the concepts and to test your hand-entered computer models.

Experienced programmers using BASIC or other languages can also use the information herein to develop software for calculating interest rates. However, all we present here for programmers are the algorithms; program listings are not included.

Part II, the final three chapters of this book, advances beyond the simple mechanics and algebra of interest rates to give you an insider's look at some closely related matters—such as taxes, inflation, and the tricks professionals use—that can greatly affect both interest rates and your financial well-being.

So pull up a computer; shall we begin?

CONTENTS

ABOUT THIS BOOK v

PART I:
The SCIENCE of Interest and Money　　　　　　　　　　**1**

1　MONEY AND THE PERSONAL COMPUTER　　　　　　　**3**

  MONEY AND THE PERSONAL COMPUTER: BACKGROUND　3
    Money Trees　3
    What Your Teachers Didn't Tell You　4
    Turning the Tables on the Pros　4
    Cast of Characters　5
    Percentage Points　7
    A Measure of Change　8
  MONEY AND THE PERSONAL COMPUTER: SUMMARY　9
  MONEY AND THE PERSONAL COMPUTER: TUTORIAL　10
    Programming Basics　10
    Spreadsheet Basics　11
    The Standard Template　13
      The Question Window　14
      The Error Section　16
      The Transformation Section　17
      The Calculation Section　18
      The Answer Window　19
    Testing Percentages　19
    Template Adjustments　20
    Template Leverage　20
  MONEY AND THE PERSONAL COMPUTER: STUDY QUESTIONS　21

2 LUMP SUMS 23

LUMP SUMS: BACKGROUND 23
   Interest Can Be Simple 23
   Interest Can Be Compounded 24
   The Math of Compound Growth 25
   Future Value 26
   Present Value 26
   The Borrower's Perspective 27
   Frequency of Compounding 28
LUMP SUMS: SUMMARY 29
LUMP SUMS: TUTORIAL 30
   Investing Lump Sums 32
   Borrowing Lump Sums 33
   Teeny-Tiny Errors 35
   Non-Money Applications 35
LUMP SUMS: STUDY QUESTIONS 37

3 EQUAL REMITTANCES 38

EQUAL REMITTANCES: BACKGROUND 38
   Present Value Annuities 39
   Future Value Annuities 40
   The Underground Stream 40
   A Future Value Annuity Example 41
   A Present Value Annuity Example 42
EQUAL REMITTANCES: SUMMARY 44
EQUAL REMITTANCES: TUTORIAL 44
   Future-Value Calculations 45
   Future-Value Problems 48
   Interest-Rate Iterations 49
   Present-Value Calculations 50
   Present-Value Problems 51
   Amortization Schedules 53
      Calculating Current Balance 53
      Calculating Interest Expense 53
EQUAL REMITTANCES: STUDY QUESTIONS 54

4 ON TO REAL LIFE 56

REAL LIFE: BACKGROUND 56
   The Bigger Template 57
   Investing in Assets 57
   Interest on Assets 58
   Liabilities 59

The Ups and Downs of Interest Rates 60
   Commitment Period 60
   Transaction Size 61
   Risk 61
   General Level of Interest Rates 62
You Be the Banker 63
Financial Strategy 101 64
REAL LIFE: SUMMARY 64
REAL LIFE: TUTORIAL 65
   The Goliah Template 65
      Year and Period 66
      Beginning Balance and Interest Amount 68
      Interest Rate/Period 68
      Remittances 69
      Yin and Yang 69
   Solving Easy Problems 69
   The Case of the Agent's Advice 72
      Wrap-Around Problem Solving 73
   The Case of the Low-Cost Lottery 76
      Period Differences 78
   The Case of the Balloon Payment 79
   The Case of ROI 81
      Discounted Cash Flow 82
      A New Publication 82
   All About @NPV 84
REAL LIFE: STUDY QUESTIONS 86

PART II
The ART of Interest and Money   87

5   DEATH, TAXES, AND INFLATION   89

DEATH, TAXES, AND INFLATION: BACKGROUND TUTORIAL 89
   Death 89
      Accounting for Fun 90
      Life Insurance 90
   Taxes 92
      The Income Tax and Investors 92
         Your Tax Bracket 92
         Tax-Free Investments 93
         Tax-Sheltered Investments 95
      The Income Tax and Borrowers 96
   Inflation 96
      Thirty Years of Fizz 97

x   Contents

        Real Interest Rates   97
        Inflation and Deflation Since 1800   98
        Interest Rates Since 1857   98
        Real Interest Rates Since 1857   101
    DEATH, TAXES, AND INFLATION: STUDY QUESTIONS   105

6   LOANS AND MORTGAGES   106

    LOANS AND MORTGAGES: BACKGROUND AND TUTORIAL   106
       Consumer Loans   106
          The Discount Method   106
          Add-On Interest   107
          Borrower Beware   108
          Credit Cards   109
             Protecting Your Cards and Your Life   110
       Commercial Loans and Real Estate Mortgages   111
          Origination Fees   111
          Offsetting Balances   112
          Buy-Downs   112
          Points   114
          Prepayment Penalties   114
          Assumptions   115
             The Hidden Value of Low-Interest Mortgages   116
          Adjustable Rate Mortgages   117
             Calculating Adjustable Rates   118
                Index and Premium Differences   118
             Teaser Rates   118
                The Math behind the Teaser   119
             Don't Bet Your House On It   120
                Tips about Caps   120
                Up in ARMs   121
          Escrow Accounts   122
       Questions to Ask about Loans and Mortgages   122
    LOANS AND MORTGAGES: STUDY QUESTIONS   123

7   INVESTMENTS   125

    INVESTMENTS: BACKGROUND AND TUTORIAL   125
       Non-Interest-Bearing Investments   125
          One Year or Three?   126
       Interest-Bearing Investments   127
          Accounts   128
             Compounding   128
             Crediting   128
             Principal Calculations   129
             Time Calculations   129
             Here's Your Free Gift   130

Interest-Bearing Paper   131
   Certificates of Deposit   131
   Treasury Bills   131
      Discount Interest   132
      The Time Zone   132
   Bonds and Notes   133
      Deciphering Bond Prices   134
      Finding the True Yield of a Bond   135
      Holding to Maturing   135
      The Consequences of Selling Out   136
Income-Producing Investments   136
Backward Is Easy   137
INVESTMENTS: STUDY QUESTIONS   137

APPENDIX A
INTEREST-RATE FORMULA SUMMARY   139

APPENDIX B
HISTORICAL INTEREST AND INFLATION RATES   142

APPENDIX C
FURTHER READING   149

GLOSSARY   151

INDEX   157

PART I
THE SCIENCE OF INTEREST AND MONEY

PART 1

THE SCIENCE OF INTEREST AND MONEY

MONEY AND THE PERSONAL COMPUTER

MONEY AND THE PERSONAL COMPUTER: BACKGROUND

Money Trees

Imagine a grove of money trees. Their roots are hard and brown like copper pennies, their stalks and branches have the coolness of silver, their leaves—at least here in the United States—are green on the back (money trees in other countries have leaves of other, and sometimes many, colors).

Like any other kind of tree, a money tree will bear fruit. You can pick this fruit and spend it, or you can sow it and grow another money tree. The baby tree will be smaller than its mother, but it, too, will bear money fruit.

This fruit is called interest.

You can uproot one of your money trees, convert it to cash, and stick the cash in your pocket. Cash in your pocket will not bear fruit, but it can be used to buy the necessities and luxuries of life. And what you buy may give you sustenance, may give you pleasure, or may bear other types of fruit for you.

Whenever you take cash from your pocket and loan or invest it, you create a money tree. When you borrow money, on the other hand, you become the energy fueling someone else's money tree. The adage "money doesn't grow on trees" is correct—the trees bear money all right, but it gets put there by borrowers.

If I were to say that it is always better to have your own money tree than to be the fuel for someone else's, you might say "That is obvious." Obvious, perhaps, but not true. As we shall see later in this book, under the right circumstances, borrowings can be a spring from which great wealth flows.

What is not so obvious, but true nonetheless, is that it is always better to have a money tree *now* than in the future. A money tree in your grove will be fruitful right now. A money tree due in the future will not. A money tree's ability to earn interest creates *time value*. We'll look into this concept at length in the next chapter.

What Your Teachers Didn't Tell You

In Shakespeare's *Hamlet*, a lord named Polonius gives his son, who is leaving for an extended stay abroad, the following advice:

Neither a borrower nor a lender be;
For loan oft loses both itself and friend,
And borrowing dulls the edge of husbandry.

The play does not record whether Laertes took his father's advice. Fortunately for the authors of books about interest rates, no one else does. Everyone you and I know is either a borrower or a lender—most of us, in fact, are *both*.

We lend money when we deposit our paychecks in a bank, when we invest in an IRA (Individual Retirement Account), even, in a sense, when we make an advance payment for a *National Geographic* subscription.

We borrow money when we use a credit card, when we finance a car, when we mortgage the house or farm.

All of us, every day, participate in financial transactions that have time value. But few of us understand the time value of money. Fewer still know how to calculate the time value of a specific transaction. We simply don't know how to compare potential investments or borrowings.

"I went to high school," you may say. "I went to college. Why didn't anyone ever teach me this stuff?"

The reason is simple. Time value calculations involve math—lots of it. The pencil and paper calculations necessary to compare two financial alternatives are time consuming and prone to error. Nobody does it that way.

Turning the Tables on the Pros

For years, financial professionals have used books of financial tables to simplify their calculations. The hard math is done by the books' authors.

Users of the books simply have to find the numbers from the right places in the right tables and use them in the right way in their calculations. Even today this is how many bankers, brokers, and other financial professionals operate. But this method requires both an insider's knowledge of how to use the tables and a copy of the tables themselves; consequently, it works well for the professionals but leaves the rest of us at an extreme disadvantage.

Enter the personal computer. This device, now appearing in homes and offices around the world, justifies the odds. Even an inexpensive personal computer can do the hard math of time-value calculations, with perfect accuracy, in a split second. No tables or hand calculations are needed. All that's required is a computer, a fistful of formulas, and the understanding to ask the right questions and to recognize the meanings of the answers.

As a computer user, you can complete time-value calculations in one of two ways. The best way is to use an electronic spreadsheet program. The first and most famous of the electronic spreadsheets was VisiCalc, which went on the market in 1980; since then, various others—with names such as Multiplan, FlashCalc, SuperCalc, and The Spreadsheet—have become available. In addition, most "integrated software" packages, such as Lotus 1-2-3, AppleWorks, and Framework, also include spreadsheet modules. In this book you will find complete instructions for creating time-value templates for your spreadsheet program.

If you have a computer and an electronic spreadsheet, this small book includes everything else you need to calculate the time value of money.

Alternatively, if you are an experienced programmer, you can write your own short and simple computer programs to do the calculations. This book includes all the *algorithms*, or formulas, you will need. However, it does not include actual program listings. Our interest rate algorithms can be used with any computer language that includes the required math functions, including most versions of BASIC.

Cast of Characters

In case you are new to computers, here are some tips about the notation to help you get started. Experienced users will quickly realize that the formulas shown in this book can be typed into a computer just as they appear.

In standard computer notation, the asterisk, when used in a formula, indicates multiplication. For example:

```
6 * 2 = 12
```

The slash indicates division. For example:

```
6 / 2 = 3
```

Parentheses indicate the order in which calculations should be done. Start with the numbers in the innermost parentheses and work outward. Without parentheses, some formulas can be ambiguous. For example, how much is:

```
4 + 6 * 2 = ?
```

If you were to evaluate this expression from left to right, the way a hand calculator or most spreadsheet programs would, the answer would be $(4+6)*2 = 20$. On the other hand, if you evaluated it as most computer languages and mathematicians would, you would give precedence to multiplication over addition. Thus, the answer would be $4 + (6*2) = 16$.

Note that the answer you get depends on the order in which you evaluate the various elements in the calculation. Therefore, in this book we will *always* use parentheses to indicate the order of evaluation. If the multiplication is supposed to occur first, for example, the formula will read:

```
4 + (6 * 2) = ?
```

Readers who have recently studied algebra may remember what exponents are and how they work. Here's the scoop for the rest of you—now don't be frightened; the computer will do all the hard work.

The caret (^) is the standard computer symbol for designating exponents. An exponent simply tells the computer to multiply a number by itself a certain number of times. For example:

```
4^3 = ?        (standard math notation is 4³)
4*4*4 = 64
```

Incidentally, exponents can also be fractional, in which case they tell the computer to find the root of a number; or negative, in which case they tell the computer to calculate the reciprocal:

```
4^(1/2) = ?    (standard math notation is 4^(1/2) or √4)
    √4 = 2

      4^-2 = ?    (standard math notation is 4^-2)
1/(4^2) = ?
    1/16   = .0625
```

That is all you need to know about exponents and computer notation. Remember that the computer will do all the calculating. All you have to understand is how to type the formulas in correctly.

Percentage Points

Interest rates are usually expressed as percentages. Most of us deal with percentages every day. Nonetheless, many of us have difficulty calculating and manipulating percentages. *Cent* is derived from a Latin word that means *hundred*. "Per cent" means, literally, "per hundred." "Per cent" and "%" mean the same thing.

The fundamental use for percentages is to describe the size of something relative to the size of something else. The "something" is called the *part*. The "something else" is called the *base*. The base's size, when expressed as a percentage, is always 100.

If the Kansas City Royals have won 22 out of 40 baseball games, they have won 55 per cent of their games. If the team continues to win at exactly the same rate, by the time they have played 100 games they will have won 55 of the hundred (55 per hundred, in fact). In this example, the number of games played, 40, is the base and the number of games won, 22, is the part. A percentage calculation mathematically expands the base to 100 and the part to a percentage, in this case, 55.

If the New York Yankees had only won 20 games when the Royals had won 22, you might assume that the Royals, who had won more games, were the better team. But if New York had played only 37 games because of schedule differences, the situation would not be so clear. Which team has the better record—the Royals with 22 wins in 40 games, or the Yankees with 20 wins in 37 games?

Percentages are perfect for solving problems like this one. To calculate a percentage, you always divide the part by the base, and multiply by 100. For example:

```
(Part / base) * 100 = Per cent

(wins / games) * 100 = winning percentage

Kansas City Royals
   (22 / 40) * 100 = ?
        .550 * 100 = 55 Per cent

New York Yankees
   (20 / 37) * 100 = ?
        .541 * 100 = 54.1 Per cent
```

At this point in the season, the Royals have a slight edge over the Yankees.

It's when you multiply by 100 that you convert the calculation's result into a true percentage—a true "per hundred." Without that multiplication, the result is "per one" or, if you prefer Latin, "per unum."

In this book I'll refer to percentages expressed in the "per one" format as *decimal fractions*. This is because such numbers are usually decimals between 0 and 1, such as the .541 winning average we just calculated for the Yankees.

Don't let the term "decimal fraction" mix you up when you run into it later. Some people have trouble with the term because they think of decimals and fractions as two entirely different creatures. But, in fact, they're closely related. The fraction 1/2 is the same thing as the decimal .5, 1/4 is the same thing as .25, and 20/37 is the same thing as .541.

The term "decimal fraction" is a very important one, because when you do a calculation involving a percentage, such as 6 per cent interest, you have to divide the 6 by 100 (to get .06) before entering it in the calculation. *Mathematical calculations involving percentages always use decimal fractions in place of the actual percentages.* Once again, don't give up if this isn't immediately clear to you—the computer will take care of all the arithmetic. All you have to do is understand how to correctly enter your own numbers and the formulas I'll give you.

A Measure of Change

The decimal fraction for 100 per cent is 1.00, or, more simply, 1. While most percentages people deal with are less than 100, percentages can also be more than 100. For example, if your home town has 775 people one year and 806 the next, its new population can be expressed as a percentage of the base population. For example:

```
(new / base) * 100 = per cent

(806 / 775) * 100 = ?

1.04 * 100 = 104 per cent
```

Often in situations such as this one, people talk about the *per cent change*. This tells how large the change, by itself, is in relation to the base. One way to calculate per cent change is to subtract the base's 100 per cent from the new year's percentage. The difference is the per cent change.

Often this is done on the decimal fraction level by subtracting 1, the decimal fraction equivalent of 100 per cent. For example:

((new / base) - 1) * 100 = per cent change

((806 / 775) - 1) * 100 = ?

(1.04 - 1) * 100 = ?

.04 * 100 = 4 per cent

Per cent change is always based on the *original state* of things. People sometimes get mixed up, however, and make the new state the base. Since the new state is bigger, it seems to them to be the base of which the change is a part. But this is incorrect, because a change always occurs from a prior state, never from a new state backward.

Another mistake you will often see (but will never make again yourself) is the assertion that a change in rate from, say, 5 per cent to 7 per cent is an increase of 2 per cent. No! It is an increase of 2 *percentage points*. An increase in a percentage from 5 to 7 is an increase of 40 per cent!

Percentage, incidentally, is not another word for small. Today's cost of living can be expressed as a percentage of the cost of living in 1970 and is anything but small. Sentences like "A percentage of the pigs are in the mud" have no meaning whatsoever.

Those of you who like working with words more than math may also be interested to know that most authorities on such stuff say "per cent" is two words and "percentage" is one. Those of you who like math better have probably just been reminded why.

MONEY AND THE PERSONAL COMPUTER: SUMMARY

1. Interest is a fee for the use of money. Interest accrues over time. Thus, money, when invested or borrowed, has a time value.

2. Time-value calculations involve extensive math and are often done by reference to mathematical tables. Even this method requires an insider's knowledge of how to use the tables and a copy of the tables themselves.

3. Personal computers give everyone, insiders and outsiders alike, the ability to calculate the time-value of money quickly and easily.

MONEY AND THE PERSONAL COMPUTER: TUTORIAL

Programming Basics

As you know, this book is not designed to teach you how to write computer programs. However, the formulas presented here can be used by programmers to develop software pertaining to interest rates. All programming formulas or algorithms are presented as they would appear in a BASIC program.

For example, here is a simple BASIC program for calculating what 10 per cent of 1,000 is:

```
10 BASE=1000
20 PCT=10/100
30 PART = BASE * PCT
40 PRINT PART
```

In this simple BASIC program, the problem's data is written into the program itself in lines 10 and 20. Line 20 also converts the percentage into the required decimal fraction. Line 30 contains the actual algorithm. Line 40 prints the answer on the screen.

A more complex BASIC program would ask a user for the problem's data and would accept keyboard input, rather than requiring that the data be made part of the program itself. A more sophisticated program might also repeat the input data when printing the answer. These programming techniques are beyond the scope of this book, however. All you'll find here are the actual algorithms—the equivalent of line 30. How you get data from a user to the algorithm and from the algorithm back out to the user is up to you.

Here are BASIC algorithms for calculating per cents and per cent change:

```
PART   = BASE * PCT
BASE   = PART / PCT
PCT    = PART / BASE

NEW    = OLD * (1 + PCTCHG)
OLD    = NEW / (1 + PCTCHG)
PCTCHG = (NEW / OLD) - 1
```

Remember that pct and pctchg must be decimal fractions.

Unlike many other books, which give you a single formula and assume you have the time to solve its derivatives yourself, herein I'll show you how to solve all related problems that have a solution. That's why there are six algorithms shown above rather than just two.

Also, most of the material in each chapter's tutorial will consist of sample problems, with answers. You can use these problems and answers to test your programs and make sure the algorithms are working correctly.

Spreadsheet Basics

Just as this book will not teach you how to program in BASIC, it will not teach you how to use a spreadsheet program. You should already know how to enter labels, values, and formulas; how to move the cursor around the screen; and how to enable any special features your spreadsheet may have. This book will not teach you any of that.

What we will do in this chapter's tutorial, however, is learn to design a useful template. But first let's review what a spreadsheet program is and how it works. There are many different spreadsheet programs on the market—this introduction will serve to introduce a common vocabulary so what we do later will be clear to you no matter what kind of spreadsheet you have.

A spreadsheet program turns your computer into a giant version of an accountant's ledger pad. The pad is divided into many *columns*. Each line of the pad creates a *row*. Almost all spreadsheet programs allow you to have more than 50 columns and more than 250 rows—some allow many more. In most instances we'll use just a small portion of this space.

Not all of a spreadsheet's rows and columns will appear on your computer screen at one time. The screen is a *window* through which you can see a small portion of the whole *worksheet*. The window always displays the portion of the sheet the cursor is in—thus, by moving the cursor around, you can see any part of the worksheet you like.

Each row-column position on the spreadsheet is called a *cell*. You may type a label into a cell, or you may put a number in one. So far these electronic sheets are just like paper ones, except, perhaps, somewhat larger. A sample worksheet is shown in Figure 1.1.

In addition to labels and numbers, you can also enter a formula into a cell. This formula can refer to other cells. For example, you can enter a formula that takes the number in cell A10 (column A, row 10—some programs refer to this cell as R10C1 or Row 10, Column 1) and multiplies it by the number in cell A11. What is displayed in the formula cell is not the formula itself but the *result* of the calculation.

Figure 1.1 A Sample Worksheet

	A	B	C	D	E	F
1						
2						
3						
4						
5						
6						
7						
8						
9						
10						
11						
12						
13						
14						
15						
16						
17						
18						
19						
20						

More important, if you now change the number in cell A10 and recalculate, the result displayed in the formula cell will instantly change to reflect the new value in A10.

In addition, what's in cell A10 could itself be a formula rather than a value. Thus it's possible to split a complex formula up into small pieces and put each piece in a separate cell. That's how we'll do some of the formulas presented in this book.

After you have filled in a worksheet with labels, numbers, and formulas, you can save it on a disk. The saved file is often called a *template*. At any time you can reload it, enter new data, and have the results displayed immediately.

In this book we will use VisiCalc notation for spreadsheet formulas. Since VisiCalc was the original spreadsheet, most other programs use similar notation and include all of the original VisiCalc's features. There are likely to be some differences, however, between VisiCalc's conventions and those of your own spreadsheet program. In particular, VisiCalc uses letters to designate columns. The first column is A, the second B, and so on. Some other programs designate the columns with numbers.

We will always explain what a formula is doing, so you should have no trouble converting the formulas we show into the correct notation for your spreadsheet. In many cases, little or no conversion will be necessary.

Your spreadsheet program may have some advanced features we won't be using here. Go ahead and use them yourself if you like. We'll stick to the standard features here so that everyone will be able to follow along.

The Standard Template

We are about to create a standard template that we will use over and over again, with minor changes, to create the templates we need to solve most interest-rate problems.

At the top of our template we'll create an area for entering data. At the bottom we'll create an area for displaying results. Next we'll divide our viewing screen into two windows so that the data-entry area will be in one and the display area in the other. In the middle of our template we'll have a calculation area where all the important math will be accomplished. Once you've created your template and gotten it working, however, you will have no further need to refer to this area and it will no longer show up on your screen.

It's now time to make use of your spreadsheet program. Start it up and let's create our standard template. Since it will be used as the foundation for all further templates in this book, you will have to enter this first template before you can enter the later ones. Let's get started.

First of all, take a blank worksheet and set it up as follows:

- set the global column width to 12
- set the calculation order to "rows"
- set calculation to "manual"

A column width of 12 allows six columns to be displayed on the standard 80-character screen. All the templates in this book use six or fewer columns. If your computer displays fewer than 80 characters across the width of the screen, all six columns won't be displayed at once, but you can scroll the window back and forth across all six as needed.

The calculation order determines whether the formulas in the cells are solved row-by-row or column-by-column. *It is essential when using templates such as the ones we're about to create that the order be by rows.*

When spreadsheet calculation is set to "automatic," the entire spreadsheet is recalculated whenever a number is changed. This slows down the creation of templates. Manual recalculation will work better with our templates, anyhow, as you will see later.

THE QUESTION WINDOW

Row 2 of each template is reserved for the template's title. Since our first template's purpose is to calculate percentages, enter the word "Percentages" in row 2.

Rows 4 and 5 of each template are reserved for column headings. In later templates we will use as many as six columns. Column headings are most easily read if the labels are formatted so they appear at the right side of the cell—over the column of numbers that will appear below. Thus you should now format the cells in the first six columns (A through F) of rows 4 and 5 for right justification.

Now enter the following labels in the first three columns of row 5:

```
    base      part      pct
```

Right justify the six cells in row 7 as well. Then put a question mark in the first three, underneath the labels. From now on we'll call these the *question cells*. In row 10 enter the words "question window". At this point your template should look like Figure 1.2.

Figure 1.2   The Question Window

```
RM .____A____.____B____.____C____.____D____.____E____.____F____
1
2Percentages
3
4
5         base       part       pct
6
7          ?          ?          ?
8
9
10question window
11
12
13
14
15
16
17
18
19
20
```

Now split your screen into two horizontal windows at line 11. The upper right cell in the top window should be A1. The top window is where we will enter data, the bottom window is for results. Enter the bottom window now and scroll until row 41 is the top row in the bottom window. In row 41 enter the words "answer window". Then copy or replicate the formats and labels in rows 4 and 5 into rows 44 and 45.

In a while, when our template is finished, we will be able to enter data in the top window's question cells. In two of the three cells we will place data. In the third we will leave a question mark. The cell with the question mark is the one we want the computer to calculate.

At that point we will manually force calculation. In an instant all three numbers—including the missing one—will appear in the *answer cells* of the lower window. For example, if we wanted to know what 10 per cent of 1,000 is, our finished worksheet would look like Figure 1.3.

Note that in Figure 1.3 you can't see rows 11 though 40. This is where we will do our calculations. Let's set up that area of the template now. Start by returning to one large window. Then enter a dashed line across all six columns of rows 11, 19, 29, and 39. This divides our work area into three sections.

Figure 1.3 Screen Display of Finished Worksheet

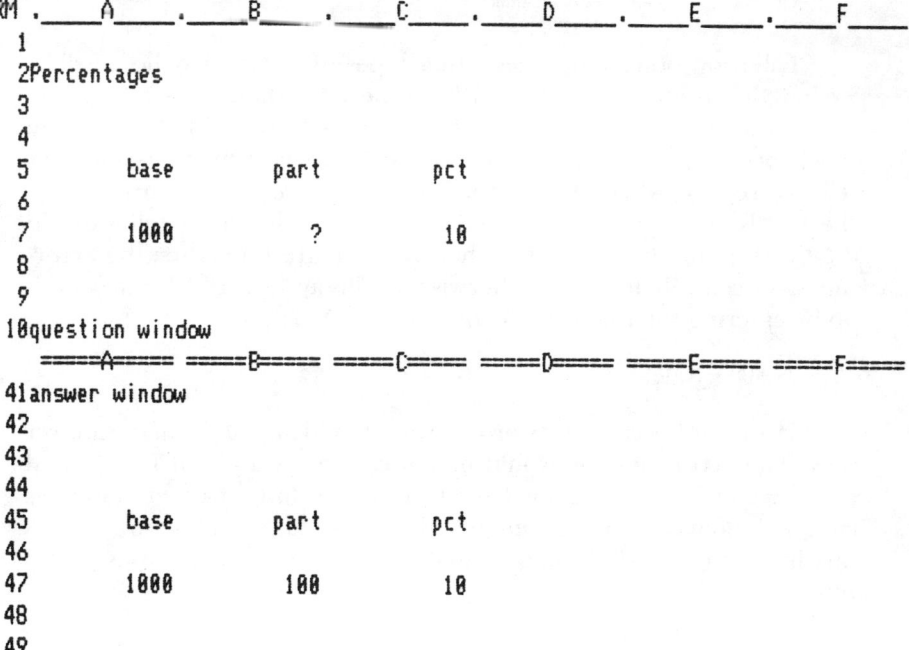

The first section will be used to catch data entry errors. In row 12, enter the word "errors". The second section will be used to transform data into the correct format. In row 20 enter the word "transformations". The third section will be used to actually calculate answers. In row 30 enter the word "calculations".

Return now to the error section. The first column of row 15 is where we'll enter our first formula.

THE ERROR SECTION

In row 15 we want to determine whether the correct amount of data has been entered in the question cells. If a user enters a number in all three question cells, there is no question left to answer. Likewise, if the user leaves question marks in more than one cell, we can't calculate an answer. In either situation we want the answer cells to say "error".

In the Percentages template, there should always be two question cells filled in with numbers. Spreadsheets have a function, called @COUNT(range), that will count how many cells in a range have numbers in them. Blank cells and cells with labels are not counted. Thus, in our case, if the count across the range of our three question cells is equal to 2, all is well. Otherwise, we have an error. The formula for cell A15 is:

```
@IF(@COUNT(A7...C7)=2,0,@ERROR)
```

Later, on other templates, other types of errors may be possible. We have left room in rows 13 and 14 to check for these errors. Later on, then, we may be using as many as three cells (A13, A14, and A15) to check for errors. It will be handy at that point to have an error-summary cell that reports whether an error is showing in *any* of the three error-check cells. All we have to do to create this error-summary cell is to add the three error-check cells together. If there are no errors, the error-summary cell will display 0; otherwise, it will say "error". We can set this up by entering the following formula in cell A17:

```
@SUM(A13...A16)
```

If an error occurs, the word "error" should appear in *all* the answer cells. The error message would be too easy to overlook if it appeared elsewhere or in only one answer cell. To make things easy on ourselves later, let's now extend the contents of cell A17 across all of row 17. Do that by putting the following formula in the other five columns of this row:

```
+A17
```

Now *test* the error section by replacing the question marks in row 7 with numbers and forcing recalculation. When there are two numbers in row 7, recalculation should change all cells in row 17 to 0. When there are some number other than two, row 17's cells should change to "error".

Again, the reason we put row 17's formula into six cells across, rather than simply into the three used by the Percentages template, is that we will revise this template later for other uses. Setting things up this way now means that when we add more question cells later, all we'll have to do is change the formula in cell A15 and everything in row 17 will continue to work correctly.

THE TRANSFORMATION SECTION

Rows 20 through 29 of our template are for data transformations. The most important transformation we need to make is one we discussed at length earlier—the transformation of a percentage into a decimal fraction.

Mathematics demands decimal fractions when working on percentage problems. Some people, on the other hand, prefer to see whole number percentages (6 per cent rather than .06). Other people, like mathematics itself, prefer to see decimal fractions. We will set up our template so that mathematics gets what it demands while you get to see your entries and results in whatever format you prefer.

Move your cursor to cell C21. If you want to enter and display percentages as decimal fractions, put a 1 here. If you prefer seeing percentages as whole per hundreds, put 100 here. (If you can't decide, use 100. The figures and test data in this book use whole-number percentages.)

Now move down to C23 and enter the following formula:

+C7/C21

The value at C23 will be the template's percentage expressed as a decimal fraction. If you decided you'd like to see decimal fractions on your template, you've put a 1 at C21. Under this arrangement, your decimal fraction percentages will be divided by 1, and hence be unchanged. If you decided on whole percentages, you should have made C21 equal 100. Doing that causes whole-number percentages to be divided by 100, and hence converted to decimal fractions. The choice is yours and is controlled by what you put at C21.

If you like, put a reminder message to the side of cell C21, such as, "1 = decimal fractions, 100 = pct". To the side of C23 you could put "pct as a decimal fraction".

THE CALCULATION SECTION

Rows 30 through 39 are for calculations. Move down to row 35. Here's where we'll put the real meat of the template. Enter the following formulas or their equivalents in row 35:

```
first column    +B7/C23
second column   +A7*C23
third column    +B7/A7
```

For any given problem, only one of these three formulas is going to provide a meaningful answer. If you leave a question mark in the third question cell, for example, the first and second formulas will give meaningless answers. This really doesn't matter, however, because we can easily sort the right answer out from the wrong ones. To do this, we once again use the *@IF* function.

In line 37, enter the following formula in the first cell:

```
@IF(@COUNT(A7)=1,A7,A35)
```

This formula tells the spreadsheet program to count how many values are in cell A7. Obviously, the most there will ever be is 1. However, if the cell contains a question mark, the count will be 0.[1]

If the count is 1, our formula will display the number you entered in the question cell. If the count is 0, indicating that this question cell is the one containing the question mark, the formula will display the contents of cell A35—our calculated answer.

Copy or replicate this formula into the next five columns now. This time the replication should be relative; that is, the formula for column B is *@IF(@COUNT(B7)=1,B7,B35)* and the formula for column F is *@IF(@COUNT(F7)=1,F7,F35)*.

Move now to cell C37. When the spreadsheet calculates the interest rate, it leaves a decimal fraction in cell C35. If you want to see whole percentages, it must be converted. The easy way to do this is to edit the formula in cell C37 so that it says:

```
@IF(@COUNT(C7)=1,C7,C35*C21)
```

---

1. At least one widely used spreadsheet program is unable to correctly count how many values are in a single cell. If this formula doesn't seem to work, try *@IF(@COUNT(A6...A7)=1,A7,A35)*.

THE ANSWER WINDOW

Now we're done with everything but the answer window. Move your cursor down to the first answer cell, A47. The cells in row 47 need a formula that adds line 17's error-checking results with line 37's calculating results. If line 17 shows an error, the answer cells should also show an error. Otherwise, line 17 will equal 0, and the answer cells should display the numbers in line 37. The correct formula for cell A47 is:

```
+A17+A37
```

Copy or replicate this formula into the other cells in row 47, again using relative positioning (+B17+B37 in column B, and so on). To keep the Percentages template pretty, you'll probably want to put the formula in only the first three columns rather than in all six.

Now move to cell A1 and once again split your screen into two windows at row 11. Put your cursor in the lower window and scroll until cell A41 is in the top-right corner. Now move the cursor back to the upper window. You are ready to enter some test data.

Testing Percentages

Once you have your spreadsheet template ready—or, if you are using the BASIC algorithms, your program ready—you should test everything to make sure it works right. Here are some sample problems, with answers, to use for test purposes. They'll also give you some examples of things you can do with percentages.

Q. Your softball team, over the course of a season, bats 810 times and gets 165 hits. What is the team batting average?
A. The base is 810 at-bats. The part is 165 hits. If you are using the spreadsheet template, put 810 under "base" and 165 under "part," leave the question mark under "pct," and force recalculation. The answer window will display 20.37 ... or .2037 ... (which depends on whether you have chosen whole-percentage or decimal-fraction display). The team batting average is .204 (in sports, averages are almost always expressed as a three-digit decimal fraction).

Q. A magazine report says your company has a 37 per cent share of the U.S. white elephant market. You know your company sells 3,500 white elephants a year. How many white elephants are sold in the U.S. by all companies put together?
A. In this problem you are looking for the base. The part is 3,500 and the per cent is 37 or .37, depending on the format you have

selected. The exact answer you should get is 9459.46; however, the magazine probably estimated the total market at 9,500.

Q. A bartender mixes one ounce of 80-proof liquor with two ounces of water. You know that 80-proof liquor is 40 per cent alcohol, but how much alcohol, in ounces, is in the drink?

A. In this problem the base is the one ounce of alcohol and the per cent is 40. The two ounces of water are just there to confuse things—they don't have anything to do with the problem. The question is how much is the part. The answer is exactly .4 ounces.

Template Adjustments

If you are a spreadsheet user, try setting your program back to automatic calculation as you test the template. I don't like automatic calculation, because I don't like the error messages that appear in the answer window while you enter data in the question window. You may prefer the ease of automatic recalculation, however. If so, just leave it on.

Another change you might find helpful is to limit the number of decimal places displayed in the answer cells. One way you can do this is by formatting the cells for dollar display, which will limit the numbers to two digits to the right of the decimal point. Some spreadsheet programs offer more flexible choices as well.

When you are comfortable that your template works as advertised, save it on a disk. You might like to create a special disk just for the templates in this book.

Template Leverage

What we have just gone through may seem like an awful lot of work for a lousy template that can't do anything but calculate percentages. But we will exploit all that effort as we create other templates.

Starting now. *After you have saved your Percentage template*, create a new Per Cent Change template by incorporating the following changes and additions:

- change title in row 2 to *Per Cent Change*
- change column headings in row 5 to:
    old   new   pct chg
- copy or replicate new headings to row 45
- in cell A35 enter +B7/(1+C23)

- in cell B35 enter *+A7*(1+C23)*
- in cell C35 enter *(B7/A7)-1*

No further modifications are necessary. Here are some test questions for checking the Per Cent Change template.

> Q. You receive a 5 per cent raise. If your old salary was $26,500 a year, what's your new salary?
> A. Old is $26,500; per cent is 5; new should be $27,825. Congratulations!
>
> Q. The number of ducks in Minnesota increases 500 per cent in one year. The new duck census shows 402,000 ducks in Minnesota. How many lived there last year?
> A. New is 402,000; per cent is 500 (or 5.00 as a decimal fraction). Last year there were 67,000 ducks in Minnesota.
>
> Q. Your bill from the power company says you pay 7.7 cents per kilowatt hour for electricity. You hear on the radio that the company has been granted an 8 per cent rate increase. Assuming you use 1,200 kilowatt hours a month, how much will your new rate per kilowatt hour be?
> A. The old rate was 7.7 cents. It will change by 8 per cent. The new rate will be 8.316 cents per kilowatt hour, no matter how much electricity you use.

Once you are sure your Per Cent Change template or program works, save it as well. We now have our foundations laid. In the next chapter we'll start investigating interest rates.

MONEY AND THE PERSONAL COMPUTER: STUDY QUESTIONS

1. Why does money have time value?
2. What do the following three symbols mean in standard computer notation: * / ^ ?
3. What is the difference between a decimal fraction and a percentage?
4. Using either the spreadsheet templates or software you have developed, calculate the answers to the following questions:
   - Teams in the Jayhawk County Softball league play a 20-game

schedule. The best team in the league won 14 of its 20 games. What per cent of its games did the team win? Another team won 45 per cent of its 20 games. How many did it win? A third team won 8 of its games—a .421 average. How many of its games were rained out and never replayed?

- The unemployment rate in a particular city rises from 7 to 8 per cent. What is the per cent change?

LUMP SUMS

LUMP SUMS: BACKGROUND

Imagine that the first boss you ever had, the one that liked you so much, dies and leaves you $1,000. Too hard to imagine? Well then, imagine you find $1,000 in the bathtub—it doesn't matter, just picture having that stack of cash in your hand.

Many people confronted with such a situation would immediately run out and spend the cash. That's great, but it doesn't do a thing for people who write books about interest rates.

You, on the other hand, as a reader of this book, might be inclined to take the cash and invest it. Perhaps you'd really like to put the money toward a Caribbean cruise, but your spouse just got a promotion and you can't do it this year. But next year, ah . . . what a trip! Meanwhile, what do you do with the cash?

Interest Can Be Simple

Being wise to the ways of interest rates, you go down to your local bank and invest in a $1,000, twelve-month certificate of deposit, or CD, with an annual interest rate of 10 per cent.

A year later you are still determined to take that cruise, so you go to the bank and redeem your CD. The bank gives you your $1,000 back, and, in addition, gives you a crisp $100 bill as interest—a fee for the use of your money. The *time value* of your $1,000 for one year, at a 10 per cent annual interest rate, is 10 per cent of $1,000—or $100. Not a bad deal, is it?

What the bank has just paid you is called *simple interest*. You invested $1,000 for one year, the bank agreed to give you 10 per cent of that amount as interest, and at the end of the year you got back both the original $1,000, which is known as the *principal*, and $100 interest.

But wait. Since we are imagining that your spouse got a promotion and is now making all kinds of money, perhaps you don't need the $1,000 back. If that's the case, you could just take the $100 interest on vacation and reinvest the original $1,000 in another CD. That way you'll have another $100 to play with next year. If you did this, you would continue to earn simple interest on your money. This could go on for generations. The key element is that you are taking the interest every year and spending it. As long as you do that you earn what's called *simple* interest.

Interest Can Be Compounded

Imagine now that your spouse is making so much money in the new job that you can reinvest the $100 interest payment along with your original $1,000 for another year. Now you will invest $1,100, and the bank will pay you $110 in interest. Continue this for seven years and you'll almost double your original $1,000, as shown in the following table:

year	beginning balance	interest earned	ending balance
1	1000.00	100.00	1100.00
2	1100.00	110.00	1210.00
3	1210.00	121.00	1331.00
4	1331.00	133.10	1464.10
5	1464.10	146.41	1610.51
6	1610.51	161.05	1771.56
7	1771.56	177.16	1948.72

Most people assume at first glance that it would take ten years of 10 per cent growth to double an investment—not seven. After all, 10 per cent interest on $1,000 earns $100 a year; $100 must be multiplied by 10 to make a second $1,000. But what such first glance assumptions don't take into account is the interest earned by reinvested interest.

Remember our grove of money trees? At the end of the first year, our original money tree bears enough money to start a second, smaller tree. At the end of the second year, *two* trees will bear fruit. Follow this analogy along and during the seventh year you have *sixty-four* money trees bearing fruit. Many of them are quite small, but they are so numerous that their fruit quickly fills bushel baskets.

When prior interest payments are reinvested, you collect what's called *compound interest*. The growth associated with such investments is often called the magic of compounding.

The Math of Compound Growth

In the last chapter we mentioned how percentages, including interest rates, are always expressed as decimal fractions (.06 rather than 6%) when used to solve a formula.

The amount of money you have at the end of any year is 100 per cent of the money you started with, plus interest. Thus, if you are earning 10 per cent interest, you can always multiply your starting principal by 110 per cent to arrive at your ending balance. Change this to decimal fractions, and what you would multiply your principal by would be *(1 + i)*, where i is the annual interest rate.

Let's let PV stand for our original lump sum principal. At the end of one year our balance would be *PV * (1 + i)*. Now take that lump-sum year-end balance and let *it* earn interest for a year—multiply it by *(1 + i)*. At the end of two years the balance would be *(PV * (1 + i)) * (1 + i)*. But, mathematically speaking, it doesn't matter which of a series of numbers you multiply together first. Thus the parentheses around the *PV * (1 + i)* can be removed.

Follow this process out a few years and here's what happens:

year	ending balance equals
1	PV * (1+i)
2	PV * (1+i) * (1+i)
3	PV * (1+i) * (1+i) * (1+i)
4	PV * (1+i) * (1+i) * (1+i) * (1+i)
••••	
	and so on

In Chapter 1 you were reminded that an exponent indicates that a number should be multiplied by itself the indicated number of times. Thus, the table we just looked at could also be written like this:

year	ending balance equals
1	PV * (1+i)^1
2	PV * (1+i)^2
3	PV * (1+i)^3
4	PV * (1+i)^4
••••	
n	PV * (1+i)^n

The last line in that table is the important one. You'll see it appear over and over again in this book. It represents the *future value* of a lump sum left to grow at compound *i*nterest for *n* years.

FUTURE VALUE

The term *future value* is an important one to get acquainted with. It is used to describe the value of an investment at some time in the future. When money is left to grow at compound interest, the future value is always larger than the starting principal (sometimes many times larger, particularly for long-term high-interest-rate investments).

However, if money is left at simple interest, where you take each year's interest and spend it, the future value is always the same as the original principal of the investment. Since you don't allow the interest to accumulate, the value of the investment doesn't grow. But if you never spend any of the principal, it won't shrink either. At simple interest, an investment's long-term future value is the same as its *present value* and never changes.

(If you *did* withdraw a portion of your principal each year, as well as interest, the future value of your investment would always be lower than its starting value and would eventually reach 0. However, the fact that you were withdrawing a portion of your funds would create a different situation, which we won't get to until the next chapter.)

PRESENT VALUE

Like *future value*, the concept of *present value* is also important. It refers to the value of a transaction when the transaction begins. When you are investing, the amount of principal you invest is the present value.

We have seen how to figure out how much money a present value will grow into if we know the interest rate and the term in years. Sometimes, however, people want to know how much they should put away now in order to have an account with a specific future value later.

For example, take that $1,000 that appeared mysteriously at the beginning of this chapter. Let's say you'd like to spend part of it right now, but you'd also like to put part of it away at compound interest where it can grow to $1,200, which you will spend on a new computer three years from now.

In this problem the future value is $1,200, the interest rate is again 10 per cent, and we have a three-year term to work with. The question is, what is the present value? How much do we have to put away now to create $1,200 later?

If *PV* represents present value, *FV* future value, *i* the annual interest rate, and *n* the number of years, then:

```
PV = FV / (1+i)^n
```

just as

```
FV = PV * (1+i)^n
```

Thus only $1200 / ((1+.10)^3)$, or $901.58, has to be invested. In three years it will grow to the required $1,200. You can take the $98.42 balance and spend it however you like.

We'll use these formulas more in this chapter's tutorial to solve some interesting everyday problems. First, though, let's investigate how borrowers see all this stuff.

THE BORROWER'S PERSPECTIVE

So far we've looked at present value and future value from the point of view of someone *investing* money. Since few of us actually inherit money from bosses or find it in the bathtub, perhaps it would be worthwhile to slip on our borrowing shoes for a page or so here.

When you are borrowing money, the present value is the amount you borrow; the future value is the amount you pay back. You can use the formula for determining future value to figure out how much you would have to pay back on a multiyear loan. For example, if you borrowed $1,000 for three years at 10 per cent interest, you would repay *1000 * ((1 +.10)^3)* or $1,331.[1]

A borrower can use the formula for present value to determine how much someone would loan now in return for a future payment. For example, if you know that when you retire in two years you will get a $2,000 bonus, but you need the money now, borrow it. The present value of $2,000, to be repaid in two years at 10 per cent interest is *2000 / ((1 +.10)^2)*, or $1,652.89.

---

[1]. Good luck. Financial institutions like it when you loan *them* money at compound interest for several years, but they hate to loan it to *anyone else* that way.

(Some people insist that the present value of such a transaction is $1,600. They calculate this by taking two years worth of 10 per cent interest out of the $2,000 you will pay back ($400). But in that situation you are paying interest on the amount of money you *pay back*, not on the amount you *borrow*. This means you'll pay more interest than the rate would indicate. Interest calculated by this method is called *discount interest*; we'll talk about it further in Chapter 6.)

Frequency of Compounding

So far, all the time-value examples we've talked about have made the rather unrealistic assumption that interest payments occur once a year. In real life they usually occur more often—semiannually, quarterly, monthly, daily, or "continuously" (hourly). The more often compounding occurs, the greater the eventual future value. It means you get those baby money trees into your orchard sooner and, as you should know by now, money has time value. The sooner those baby trees bear fruit for you, the more fruit you'll eventually have.

Let's go back to our original $1,000 and assume you invest in a six-month CD rather than a twelve-month CD. At the end of six months, at 10 per cent *annual* interest, you would get $50. To calculate this, it's necessary to adjust the interest rate from annual to interest-per-period. Thus if the period is half a year, you cut the interest rate in half. More about this in the tutorial.

Imagine now that you reinvest your original $1,000 and your $50 interest in another six-month CD. When it matures, this $1,050 CD will pay you $52.50 in interest. Thus, over the course of the year, you earn $102.50 in interest—$2.50 more than you would have gotten on an annual-payment twelve-month CD.

If you were to do the same thing with four three-month CDs, your total interest for the year would be $103.81. And if you were to buy a twelve-month CD with monthly compounding, the total interest would be $104.71. With daily compounding, the interest goes to $106.16; with continuous, to $106.17.

Financial institutions often talk about the *effective annual yield* of investments compounded more often than once a year. This is the interest rate you would have to get with a one-year simple interest investment to obtain as much actual interest as at the lower, compounded rate. Here's a table that will give you a better feel for this. It shows the effective yield of an investment at various interest rates with various compounding periods.

Effective annual yield of an investment at various
interest rates and compounding periods

	annual interest rate				
	5	10	15	20	25
compounding					
annual	5.00	10.00	15.00	20.00	25.00
semiannual	5.06	10.25	15.56	21.00	26.56
quarterly	5.09	10.38	15.87	21.55	27.44
monthly	5.12	10.47	16.08	21.94	28.07
daily	5.13	10.52	16.18	22.13	28.39
continuously	5.13	10.52	16.18	22.14	28.40

If you study this table, you'll notice that there is virtually no difference between daily compounding and continuous compounding. In fact, there is hardly any difference between monthly compounding and daily. Thus, don't be overly impressed by a financial institution's frequency-of-compounding claims.

Notice also that the effect of compounding is greater at higher interest rates than at lower. A 5¼ per cent investment with annual compounding is better than daily compounding at 5 per cent; but 28¼ per cent with annual compounding is worse than daily compounding at 25 per cent. Because of this effect, financial institutions sometimes loudly advertise daily compounding on low-interest passbook accounts while paying interest less often on high rate CDs.

LUMP SUMS: SUMMARY

1. *Present value* refers to the current value of a transaction. A borrower thinks of present value as the amount borrowed. An investor thinks of present value as the amount invested or the principal.

2. *Future value* refers to the value of a transaction at a specific time in the future. A borrower thinks of future value as the amount remaining to be repaid. An investor thinks of future value as the principal amount plus the interest it has earned.

3. *Simple interest* is interest paid on invested principal only. *Compound interest* is interest paid on both the principal and prior interest payments.

4. Compounding can occur after various periods of time. More frequent compounding increases the *effective annual yield*, which is the rate a simple-interest investment would have to earn to match the interest paid on a compounded, lower-rate investment.

LUMP SUMS: TUTORIAL

The programming algorithms for lump-sum interest-rate calculations are:

```
Where:
    PV = present value
    FV = future value
    I  = annual interest rate as a decimal fraction
    N  = number of years
    Q  = number of compounding periods per year
    I1 = I/Q = interest rate per period
    N1 = N*Q = total number of compounding periods

PV = FV / ((1+I1)^N1)
FV = PV * ((1+I1)^N1)
 I = Q * ( ((FV/PV)^(1/N1)) - 1 )
 N = (1/Q) * (LOG(FV/PV)/LOG(1+I1))
      (these logarithms can be either
       common (LOG10) or natural (LOGe))
 Q cannot be determined by formula
```

Spreadsheet users should make the following changes to either of the percentages templates:

<u>question window</u>
- change title in row 2 to <u>Time Value of a Lump Sum</u>
- change column headings in rows 4 and 5 to:

    present   future   annual   years   compound-
    value   value   interest   ings/year

- place question marks in cells D7 and E7
- in cell E8 enter and right justify <u>?=error</u>

<u>error section</u>
- in cell A13 enter <u>@IF(@COUNT(E7)=1,0,@ERROR)</u>
- edit formula in cell A15 to <u>@IF(@COUNT(A7...D7)=3,0,@ERROR)</u>

transformation section
- in cell C27 enter +C23/E7
- in cell D27 enter +D7*E7

calculation section
- in cell A32 enter (1+C27)^D27
- in cell A35 enter +B7/A32
- in cell B35 enter +A7*A32
- in cell C33 enter +D32^(1/D27)
- in cell C35 enter (C33-1)*E7
- in cell D32 enter +B7/A7
- in cell D33 enter @LOG10(D32)/@LOG10(1+C27)
- in cell D35 enter D33/E7
- in cell E35 enter +E7

answer window
- copy or replicate column headings to rows 44 and 45

The question window now has five question cells. Because of some mathematical complexities, however, it is impossible to calculate directly the number of compoundings a year. Consequently, the "compoundings/year" question cell must always have data in it. That's why we put the little message below it that says, in shorthand, that a question mark in this cell will return an error.

In the error section we add a new formula in cell A13 that checks to make sure that the compoundings-per-year question cell has been filled in. We also edit cell A15 so that the formula there looks in four question cells instead of three, and so that it expects to find data in three of the four.

In the transformation section, we add two new transformations. Cell C27 will hold the interest rate per compounding period from now on. This figure is calculated by dividing the annual interest rate by the number of compounding periods per year. Cell D27 will hold the total number of compounding periods; this value is calculated by multiplying the number of years by the number of compounding periods per year.

A number of changes must be made in the calculation section. In cell A32 we enter the spreadsheet equivalent of $(1 + i)^n$. This cell is then used to calculate both present value in cell A35 and future value in cell B35. The additions to column C and column D calculate the interest rate and the number of years. It is also necessary to bring the number of compounding periods entered in cell E7 down to cell E35.

The only change we need to make in the answer window is to update the column headings.

Investing Lump Sums

Once you have made the foregoing changes to your spreadsheet template or written a program around the algorithms given, you're ready to test your work with the following data. (Don't forget to *save* the template when you are satisfied it works right. Our next templates will be based on this one.)

Q. You don't know it yet, but the day you were born your grandfather invested $1,000 in a special trust for you. You will find out about the trust on your 65th birthday and will have complete access to the funds at that time. The trust's money is in an investment that pays 3 per cent annually, compounded quarterly. How much will the trust be worth on your 65th birthday? How much would it be worth if the investment was at 4 per cent? at 5 per cent? at 10 per cent?
A. The present value is $1,000. The future value is unknown. The number of years is 65 and the number of compoundings per year is 4. At 3 per cent, the trust will be worth $6,977.73 on your 65th birthday; at 4 per cent, $13,290.98; at 5 per cent, $25,275.98; at 10 per cent, $614,051.35. As you can see, the rate of interest you earn *does* make a difference.

Q. You would like to set up a trust like the one mentioned in the last question for your own newborn grandchild. You would like the trust to be worth $100,000 and you can get 7.5 per cent interest compounded semiannually. How much do you have to invest? How much would you have to invest with quarterly compounding? With monthly? With daily?
A. The present value is unknown. The future value in $100,000. The interest rate is 7.5 per cent. The number of years is again 65. With semiannual compounding (2 compoundings per year), you would have to invest $834.73; with quarterly (4), $798.76; with monthly (12), $775.18; with daily (365), $763.89.

Q. As a bonus, you receive an option to buy 100 shares of your company's stock at $10 per share any time within the next seven years. If you put $500 away right now in an account that is compounded annually, what interest rate must you earn in order to accrue enough money to buy the stock?
A. The present value is $500. The future value is 100 * 10 (spreadsheet users: you can enter it just like that in the question cell of your spreadsheet—no need to multiply it out in your head). The annual interest is unknown. The number of years is 7 and the number of

compoundings per year is 1. A rate of 10.41 per cent or higher will turn your $500 into $1,000 or more within seven years.

Q. How long does it take monthly compounding to double your money at 5 per cent interest? at 10 per cent? at 15 per cent? at 20 per cent?
A. Use 1 for present value and 2 for future value (any numbers will work as long as future value is two times present value). Put 12 in compoundings per year. At 5 per cent, double-your-money takes 13.89 years; at 10 per cent, 6.96 years; at 15, 4.65; at 20, 3.49.

Q. Is your money better off in an account that pays 6 per cent interest compounded daily or 6-1/4 per cent compounded semiannually?
A. Since no specific present value is given, use $1,000. You could use any present value, but 1,000 is large enough to show an effect and is also nice and round. Assume one year—this, too, could be anything. The future value is what we want to know; put a question mark in that cell. To test the first case, enter 6 under annual interest and 365 (days per year) under compoundings per year. The future value of this investment is $1,061.83. To test the second case, enter 6.25 under annual interest and 2 under compoundings per year. The future value of this investment is slightly better, $1,063.48.

Borrowing Lump Sums

In the borrowing questions that follow, the terms of the loans will be less than one year. This presents a special problem, in that the financial world has no *standard* technique for calculating the length of short time periods. It may seem quite clear, for example, that a quarter of a year should be expressed as .25, but some people use 90/365 (.246 . . .) for the January-March quarter, 91/365 (.249 . . .) for the April-June quarter, and 92/365 (.252 . . .) for the July-September and October-December quarters. The differences are due to the actual number of days in each quarter. Some of these very same people will divide by 366 and use 91 for the number of first-quarter days during leap years, others will forget this.

As if this isn't enough, some institutions divide by 364 or even 360 days per year. Some calculate all months as having 30 days. Some say six months is half a year and some say it depends which months you're talking about. We'll discuss these differences further in Chapter 7. For now, let's assume that a quarter of a year is .25 years and that 30 days is 30/365ths of a year.

The template and programming algorithms we're working with in this chapter are designed to calculate compound interest. However, they can also calculate simple interest quite easily. For simple interest, the number of compounding periods per year must be made proportional to the term of the loan. For example, a one-year loan would have one compounding period, a half-year loan two periods, a quarter-year loan four periods. Programmers can say $Q=1/N$ when working with simple interest; spreadsheet programmers can enter $1/D7$ in question cell E7.

Now let's solve some problems.

Q. Your business borrows $75,000 on September 15 to pay for Christmas season inventories. The loan's term is one quarter—it will be paid back in mid-December. The interest rate is 15 per cent. How much will be paid back?

A. The present value is $75,000. The future value is unknown. The annual interest is 15 per cent, the term .25 years, the number of compounding periods per year 4. Your business will have to pay back $77,812.50.

Q. Your toy firm receives an order for 12,200 stuffed bears at $4.65 each. The bears must be delivered four months from today; you will be paid two months after that. Your banker will loan you the present value of the payment today at 12.5 per cent interest. With that money in hand, your total cost of production and marketing will be $4.00 per bear. How much, per bear, will you make on the order? How much will the bank get? What if the bank were charging 15 per cent? 17.5 per cent?

A. We don't know yet how much the bank will actually lend, so put a question mark in the present value cell. Since the problem asks for the answer on a per-bear basis, let's ignore the size of the order and just enter $4.65 as the future value—the amount, per bear, we will pay the banker back in six months. The term is .5 years and the number of compounding periods per year is 2. At 12.5 per cent, the bank would lend you $4.38 per bear. You'd make 38 cents per bear and the bank would get 27 cents in interest. At 15 per cent interest, the bank would lend you $4.33 per bear, you'd make 33 cents, the bank would get 32 cents. At 17.5 per cent, the bank would lend you $4.28 per bear; you'd make 28 cents, the bank would get 37 cents.

Q. You had to borrow $10 from your office mate the day you left your purse in the car. A week later you remembered to pay her back

and you bought her a 50-cent Coke in return for the favor. What rate of interest did you pay on the loan?
A. The present value is $10. The future value is $10.50. The term is 7/365, and the number of periods per year is 365/7. The annual interest rate is 260 per cent!

Teeny-Tiny Errors

As you become proficient at calculating the time value of money, you will notice that the answers you arrive at are sometimes a few cents or a few hundredths of a percentage point different from the answers of the professionals you deal with. (And perhaps from this book!) These small differences are caused by rounding errors.

Calculate 1/3 and display or print it. (If you are using a spreadsheet, temporarily widen the column you typed *1/3* in to 25 characters or so). Now count the number of digits shown as a result of the calculation. This is the number of digits of *precision* your spreadsheet program or programming language can handle. (Note: Precision is a function of *software*. Expensive computers have the capability to process high-precision numbers faster than small computers, but whether or not they actually do depends on the software you are using.)

In the books the financial pros use, the tables usually have six or seven digits to the right of the decimal point. Almost any spreadsheet program can calculate with more precision than that. Usually, then, your answer will be the more precise one, but as long as the difference is clearly rounding error, make life easy and let the professional use his or her figures.

Most computer languages and spreadsheet programs have plenty of precision for typical time-value calculations. However, if you intend to deal in securities in lots of $1,000,000 and higher, you may find it worthwhile to spend the extra money for high-precision software and faster computers.

Non-Money Applications

The lump-sum time-value calculations we've studied in this chapter are mostly just a stepping stone on the way to true interest-rate understanding. Most of the time-value problems you'll run into in real life do not involve lump sums, but instead involve a series of payments or deposits. We'll study these kinds of transactions further in the next two chapters.

In the meantime, however, it's worth knowing that lump-sum compound growth has many applications outside of interest rates. You may find your new understanding helpful as you study any phenomena that has compound growth, whether it is your own salary, the world's population, or the national defense budget.

In these kinds of problems, you will almost always use one compounding per year. Here are some sample non-interest-rate problems you may find interesting.

Q. Five years ago your company's revenues were $1.2 million. This year they will be $2.6 million. What is your company's *annual growth rate*?

A. Many people try to solve this problem by finding the per cent change between the two figures and dividing by five. This method would give you an annual growth rate of 23 per cent. However, it is incorrect, because if you increase $1.2 million by 23 per cent five times, you get revenues of $3.38 million for the current year, not $2.6 million. The correct solution is to use our Time Value of a Lump Sum formulas. The present value is $1.2 million, the future value is $2.6 million, the term is 5 years. The true annual growth rate is 16.7 per cent.

Q. In 1970 the world's population was about 3,610 million. In 1980 it was about 4,432 million. What was the population's annual growth rate during this decade? If population continues to grow at this rate, what will the world's population be in the year 2000?

A. For the first part of this question, the present value is 1970's 3,610 million. The future value is 4,432 million. The term is 10 years. The annual growth rate for the decade then calculates out as 2.07 per cent. To answer the second part of the question, enter this percentage in the annual-interest question cell. Make the present value 1980's 4,432 million. Put a question mark in the future-value cell. The term is 20 years. In the year 2000 the world's population would be 6,677 million if this growth rate continued.

Q. In fiscal 1975, the Department of Defense was given authority to spend $86,585 million. For fiscal 1985, President Reagan asked Congress to give the department $313,375 million. What was the annual rate of growth in the defense budget during these 10 peacetime years?

A. Use $86,585 million as the present value, $313,375 million as the future value, and 10 years as the term. The annual rate of growth in the U.S. defense budget during this period was about 13.7 per cent.

LUMP SUMS: STUDY QUESTIONS

1. What's the difference between simple interest and compound interest?

2. When you invest a lump sum, what is the present value equivalent to? the future value?

3. When you borrow a lump sum, what is the present value equivalent to? the future value?

4. What effect does compounding have on the effective annual yield of an investment?

5. What is a $1,000, quarterly compounded investment worth after 5, 10, 15, 20, 25, and 30 years at the following rates of interest: 5 per cent? 7.5 per cent? 10 per cent? 12.5 per cent?

6. In 1876, the U.S. gross national product was about $24 billion (1972 dollars). In 1976 it was $1,298 billion. What was the average yearly growth rate in the gross national product over the period?

EQUAL REMITTANCES

EQUAL REMITTANCES: BACKGROUND

Most interest-rate problems involve a series of payments or deposits—remittances we'll call them—rather than just the lump sums we looked at in Chapter 2. Typical examples are car loans and home mortgages, where, in return for a lump sum now, you make a series of equal monthly payments. Or you might make a series of deposits into a pension fund or an IRA in return for a lump-sum value in the future.

A series or stream of remittances is often called an *annuity* (said uh-NEW-ity). This word has the same root as the word *annual*. Many dictionaries, in fact, define an annuity as a series of annual payments, although the word is commonly used to describe weekly, monthly, and other kinds of payments as well.

In its most general sense, the word annuity can denote any old stream of remittances—the weekly allowance you got as a kid, for example. But the lawyers, accountants, and life insurance agents you meet in everyday life usually mean something very specific when they use it. The problem is they all mean something slightly different.

"Annuity" is a gelatinous little word that professionals slip and slide all over the place to suit their own interests. Make sure you understand its exact meaning when the ramifications will be important to you. The meaning of annuity used in this book is a common one. But your own lawyer or accountant or life insurance agent may mean something slightly different. Don't be afraid to ask.

In this book, an *annuity* is a series of equal remittances that is either redeeming an initial transaction or being amassed for a final transaction.

At one end of an annuity is a lump sum. When you borrow money to buy a car, the lender provides you with a lump sum in return for your series of remittances. When you invest in an IRA, you make a series of remittances so that you will have a lump sum of money available when you retire.

At the other end of an annuity is nothing. Your payments into an IRA start with nothing. When your loan payments end, you owe nothing.

Thus, there are two different types of annuities. One type has a lump-sum present value and a future value of 0. In this book we'll refer to this type of annuity as a *present value annuity*. The second type of annuity has a present value of 0 and a lump-sum future value. We'll call this type a *future value annuity*. The name we give each type reflects where the lump sum lies.

Present Value Annuities

Both borrowings and investments can form the basis of a present value annuity. Again, a typical example of this type of transaction is the monthly payment home mortgage. A lender provides you with a lump sum of cash you can use to purchase a home. You pay off the loan with a series of equal monthly payments over a period of many years. After you make the final payment you owe nothing.

On the investment side, you can invest a single lump sum and withdraw the sum and the interest it collects in a series of remittances over a number of years until nothing is left. People near retirement, who may have a lump sum to invest (usually made up of savings, life insurance, and pension funds) and a need for monthly income, are more likely to execute this type of transaction than the rest of us, although it has several other uses as well.

The essential characteristic of a present value annuity is that its future value is always *lower than* its present value. In the transactions we looked at in Chapter 2, this was never the case. In the examples we considered there, when a lump sum was allowed to grow at compound interest, the sum's future value was always *higher than* its present value. In Chapter 2 we also briefly discussed what happens when the interest earned by a lump sum is immediately spent; we saw that the sum's future value is always *equal to* its present value. This is because nothing is ever added to or taken away from the sum.

But with a present value annuity, each remittance not only represents simple interest earned, but also a portion of the original lump sum.

Thus, this type of annuity always has a future value *lower than* its present value. And its future value always eventually reaches 0.

Future Value Annuities

Just as with present value annuities, both borrowings and investments can form the basis of a future value annuity. It is easy to get mixed up and think that one type of annuity is associated only with loans and other type only with investments, but this isn't correct.

Investors use the mathematics of future value annuities to determine how much a series of remittances left to grow at compound interest would be worth at some point in the future. A typical future value annuity is a monthly payroll deposit into your credit union.

It is unusual for an individual to borrow a little bit every month and pay it back in a lump sum, but it can be done. A *reverse annuity mortgage* is a financing option designed for older people who have property but little cash. Rather than selling their homes, retired people can arrange for a monthly payment that accrues as a loan secured by the house. The loan is repaid with interest when the homeowner moves or dies and the house is sold.

In addition, borrowing a little bit every month for lump sum repayment is something financial institutions do every day. Life insurance companies use the mathematics of future value annuities to determine how much you have to pay each year for various amounts of insurance. The insurance company "borrows" a periodic remittance from you in exchange for a lump sum it has committed to pay to your beneficiary at some time in the future.

Future value annuities always have a present value of 0. Before you make the first remittance, the transaction has no value. This is an essential difference between future value and present value annuities. With present value annuities, a lump sum amount changes hands before the first remittance.

The Underground Stream

Mathematically speaking, both a lump-sum present value and a lump-sum future value can be calculated for any stream of remittances. Since it *can* be done, some people get mixed up and think it *should* be done—even some professionals. But you know better. If the stream of remittances represents a present value annuity, the future-value calculation is meaningless, because the true future value of the transaction is 0. Likewise, if the stream represents a future value annuity, a present-value calculation is nonsense; the true present value is 0.

Imagine, for a moment, the special case in which you deposit $10,000 at 10 per cent interest for five years and withdraw it in equal installments. As you receive each installment, you immediately deposit it in a second account that earns 10 per cent interest. How much will the second account be worth at the end of five years?

This problem can be solved with the simple lump-sum calculations we studied in Chapter 2. The fact that you are taking a stream of remittances out of one account and immediately directing it into a second account makes the annuities *cancel each other out*. When you have a lump sum on both ends of the transaction and two annuities with equal interest rates, the annuities become transparent. You can solve the problem with simple lump-sum calculations.

A Future Value Annuity Example

Let's take a look at some examples that show how annuities work. To keep things simple, we'll assume an interest rate of 10 per cent, with interest calculated once a year.

Let's look first at a future value annuity, since it is the easier type to understand. You deposit $1,000 in an IRA every year. What is the future value of the IRA?

A Sample Future Value Annuity
interest rate = 10%

	starting balance	int earned	remit- tance	ending balance
year 1	0	0	1000	1000
year 2	1000	100	1000	2100
year 3	2100	210	1000	3310
year 4	3310	331	1000	4641
year 5	4641	464	1000	6105

The "starting balance" column of this table shows how much the IRA is worth at the beginning of each year. The last column shows the ending balance—how much the IRA is worth at year-end. The figures for each year run across the table.

Each year, interest is earned on the starting balance. In year 1, the starting balance is 0; thus, no interest is earned. The first remittance is made at the end of the first year.

In dealing with standard annuities, *it is always assumed that remittances are made at the end of the period.*

In year 2, the starting balance is the $1,000 ending balance of year 1. This amount earns 10 per cent interest—$100—during the second year. At the end of the second year a second $1,000 remittance is made. The ending balance is calculated by adding these three items—beginning balance, interest earned, and remittance—together. The total at the end of the second year is $2,100.

In the third year, $210 of interest is earned, and so on through year 5. Note that the balance at the end of the fifth year is $1,105 higher than the total of the five remittances—$6,105 compared to $5,000. This represents interest earned by the remittances and interest earned by retained interest. The magic of compounding is at work.

The ending balance for each year is also the future value of a $1,000 10-per cent annuity of that many years' duration. For example, a one-year $1,000 10-per cent annuity has a future value of $1,000, a two-year annuity has a future value of $2,100, a three-year $3,310, and so on; you could extend the table out any number of years. Obviously, the future value of an annuity depends on the length of the annuity—on how many remittances are in the stream.

To determine the future value of a stream of remittances, you need to know the size of the remittance, how often remittances are made, the interest rate, and the term of the annuity (the number of remittances). We'll look at the actual calculations in this chapter's tutorial.

A Present Value Annuity Example

Now let's look at a present value annuity. In this example, a five-year stream of $1,000 payments is resulting from a five-year, 10-per cent investment. The amount of the initial investment—the present value of the annuity—was $3,791.

A Sample Present Value Annuity
interest rate = 10%

	starting balance	remittance	interest earned	principal redeemed	ending balance
year 1	3791	1000	379	621	3170
year 2	3170	1000	317	683	2487
year 3	2487	1000	249	751	1736
year 4	1736	1000	174	826	909
year 5	909	1000	91	909	0

Again, each row of the table shows what happens during one year of the annuity. In the first row, we start with a balance of $3,791. At the end of the year we earn 10 per cent of that amount, $379, as interest. Thus, $379 of our remittance comes from interest earned. The rest, $621, comes out of the flesh of our investment.

By subtracting this $621 from the investment's beginning balance of $3,791, we can calculate its year-end balance of $3,170. This amount is carried forward and is the beginning balance for the second year. (Note, once again, that when standard annuities are being dealt with, it is assumed that remittances are made at the end of the period.)

Note that each year we earn *simple* interest on the outstanding investment. There is no compounding here; no interest-on-interest. As the years go by, the outstanding investment declines; thus the interest earnings also decline. In order to keep the remittances equal we must redeem more of the original investment each year.

With very long term transactions, such as a 30-year home mortgage, early remittances consist almost entirely of interest. For example, a 30-year, 10 per cent, $100,000 home mortgage would have payments of $877.57 per month. About 95 per cent of the first monthly payment, $833.33 of the $877.57, would go to pay interest on the $100,000. The rest of the remittance, $44.24, would lower the amount of the loan itself, but just ever so slightly. Thus, during the second month, the amount owed (and collecting interest) would still be $99,955.76.

The following table shows how the monthly payments split up at the fifth, tenth, fifteenth, twentieth, and twenty-fifth years of a such a mortgage:

A Sample 30-Year Fixed-Rate Home Mortgage
interest rate = 10%

first payment of	starting balance	remit- tance	interest paid	principal paid	interest as pct of remittance
1st year	100,000.00	877.57	833.33	44.24	95%
5th year	96,574.16	877.57	804.78	72.79	92%
10th year	90,937.87	877.57	757.82	119.75	86%
15th year	81,664.43	877.57	680.54	197.03	78%
20th year	66,406.75	877.57	553.39	324.18	63%
25th year	41,303.16	877.57	344.19	533.38	39%

The process of paying off a debt with a stream of remittances is called *amortization*. This home mortgage table is an abbreviated *amortization table*. A complete amortization table has a line for each remittance made during the life of the loan and shows the remittance, the interest charge, the principal repayment, and the balance outstanding. You'll learn how to construct such a table in this chapter's tutorial.

EQUAL REMITTANCES: SUMMARY

1. Most interest-rate problems involve a series of periodic payments or investments. A stream of such remittances can be called an *annuity*.

2. In a *present value annuity*, a lump sum of money changes hands before any remittances are made. A typical example of a present value annuity is a home mortgage.

3. In a *future value annuity*, a lump sum of money will change hands after all remittances have been made. A typical example of a future value annuity is a retirement account.

4. The future value of a present value annuity is 0. Likewise, the present value of a future value annuity is 0.

5. With standard annuities it is assumed that remittances are made at the *end* of the period.

6. The process of paying off a loan with a stream of remittances is called *amortization*.

EQUAL REMITTANCES: TUTORIAL

The calculations for determining the present value and future value of a stream of remittances are similar to the calculations we did with lumps sums in Chapter 2. The equations have only two new variables: the amount of the remittance and the number of remittances per year.

In many annuities, interest is calculated whenever a remittance is made. Thus the number of remittances and the number of compoundings per year are the same. In fact, the tables the professionals use usually assume this is the case. With a home mortgage, for example, remittances are usually made monthly. Interest is calculated and paid with each remittance.

In other situations, however, this is not the case. For example, you might make a *weekly* deposit into your credit union, where interest is compounded *quarterly*. The formulas provided in this chapter, unlike the tables the professionals use, can handle this kind of situation easily.

In Chapter 2's lump-sum calculations, it was possible to determine an unknown interest rate when the present value, future value, number of years, and compoundings per year were known. You might remember, however, that because of mathematical complexities, it was impossible to calculate an unknown number of compoundings per year when everything else was known. (Spreadsheet users: Remember the *? = error* we put under the compoundings per year question cell?)

Those same mathematical complexities now throw their shadows over the interest rate as well. There is no *formula* that can determine the interest rate when everything else about an annuity is known. This is unacceptable, since it is often critical to determine the interest rate a transaction offers. Though it can't be done by formula, it can be done with a process called *iteration*. We'll study the procedure fully in this tutorial.

First let's look at the calculations associated with future value annuities. Then we'll investigate how to discover a missing interest rate with iteration. Finally we'll study the calculations associated with present value annuities. Let's get started.

Future-Value Calculations

The programming algorithms for determining the future value of a stream of remittances are:

```
Where:
    FV = future value
   PMT = remittance amount
     I = annual interest rate as a decimal percentage
     N = number of years
     Q = number of compounding periods per year
     U = number of remittances per year

    I1 = I/Q = interest rate per period
    N1 = N*Q = total number of compounding periods
    Q1 = Q/U = compounding periods per remittance period

    T1 = temporary intermediate variable
    T2 = temporary intermediate variable
    T3 = temporary intermediate variable
    T4 = temporary intermediate variable

T1 = (1+I1)^N1
T2 = (1+I1)^Q1
T3 = (T1-1) / (T2-1)
```

```
FV  = PMT * T3
PMT = FV / T3
T4  = (FV/PMT) * (T1-1)
N   = (1/Q) * (LOG10(1+T4) / LOG10(1+I1))
      (these logarithms can be either
       common (LOG10) or natural (LOGe))

I, Q, and U cannot be determined by formula
```

Spreadsheet users can create a template for determining the future value of a stream of remittances by modifying slightly the template developed in Chapter 2:

- load the <u>Time Value of a Lump Sum</u> template

  <u>question window</u>

- change title in row 2 to <u>Future Value of a Series of Remittances</u> (Present Value=0)

- change column headings in rows 4 and 5 to:

future	remittance	pct	years	compound-	remit-
value	amount	interest		ings/year	tances/yr

- place a question mark in cell F7

- enter and right justify <u>?=error</u> in cells C8 and F8

  <u>error section</u>

- edit formula in cell A13 to
  @IF(@COUNT(C7,E7,F7)=<u>3</u>,0,@ERROR)

- edit formula in cell A15 to
  @IF(@COUNT(A7,B7,D7)=<u>2</u>,0,@ERROR)

  <u>transformation section</u>

- in cell F27 enter <u>+E7/F7</u>

  <u>calculation section</u>

- in cell B32 enter <u>((1+C27)^F27)</u>

- in cell A33 enter <u>(A32-1) / (B32-1)</u>

- in cell A35 enter <u>+B7*A33</u>

- in cell B35 enter <u>+A7/A33</u>
- in cell D32 enter <u>(A7/B7)*(B32-1)</u>
- edit formula in cell D33 to @LOG10(<u>1+</u>D32)/@LOG10(1+C27)
- blank out cells C33 and C35

   <u>answer window</u>
- copy or replicate column headings from rows 4 and 5 to rows 44 and 45
- copy or replicate (relative) cell E47 to F47

In the question window we change the title and the column headings, add a question cell in the sixth column, and place *?=error* under the question cells for interest rate, compoundings per year, and remittances per year to show that these values can't be directly calculated.

The error section is modified so that an *error* is reported if any of the question cells that can't be calculated are left empty. The formula that counts the number of question cells with data in them must be slightly modified also, since interest rates can no longer be calculated directly.

In the transformation section we add a formula that yields the number of compoundings per number of remittances.

The most extensive template modifications occur in the calculation section. Our old friend *(1+i)^n* in cell A32 now has a similar formula next to it in cell B32. The difference between the two cells is the value used for *n*. In A32 we use the total number of compounding periods as our exponent. In B32 *n* is the number of compoundings per number of remittances.

Several other changes are made in columns A, B, and D. The formulas formerly in column C, which calculated an unknown interest rate when all other values were known, no longer work and should be removed.

Note that the formulas in row 37 of columns C, E, and F have formulas that refer to empty cells in row 35. These formulas are "wrong." However, they do not need to be changed because row 35 is only used when the corresponding question cell holds a question mark. But the cells in columns C, E, and F aren't allowed to hold question marks; if a question mark does appear in one of these question cells, our error section will put *error* in all six answer cells. Thus the "wrong" formulas are of no consequence and can be left as is.

Finally, the answer window must be changed to reflect the new column headings and the new answer cell in the sixth column.

Once you have created this new template, save it (use a new name—don't overwrite your lump-sum template), test it, and resave it if necessary. Later in the chapter we'll modify this template for use with present value annuities.

Future-Value Problems

Now let's look at some typical problems that will test your spreadsheet or, if you are a programmer, your program.

Q. Many financial institutions like to show you how much an individual retirement account will be worth in the future. If you deposit $2,000 a year in a 10-per cent, quarterly compounded IRA for 10 years, how much will you have after the tenth deposit?

A. In this problem, the unknown is the future value of the transaction. The remittance is $2,000, the interest rate is 10 per cent, the number of years is 10, the compoundings per year is 4, and the remittances per year is 1. Crank that through your computer and you should find a future value of $32,463.48.

Note—Annuity calculations, including the ones given here, usually assume that *remittances are made at the end of the period,* as discussed earlier in this chapter. Thus, future value annuity calculations assume that *no interest is earned in the first period.* Yet in real life an IRA starts earning interest at the time of the first deposit. The above question is phrased accordingly, "How much would you have after the tenth deposit?" Although you should use 10 as the number of years, be aware that only nine years actually pass between the first deposit and the tenth. If you intend to take your money out at the *end* of the tenth year, the calculated future value must be increased to reflect the interest earned during the tenth year. To do this, use 11 for the number of years and subtract the final remittance, which won't be made, from the calculated future value. Thus the future value after 10 full years would be $35,833.60. (Exactly one $2,000 remittance less than the $37,833.60 your computer should calculate for an 11-year annuity.)

Q. On his fourteenth birthday, your son says he wants to save up so he can buy a car when he turns 18. Assuming he will make weekly deposits into a 5¼ per cent, daily compounded savings account, how much must he deposit each week to save $2,500 for a used car?

A. The future value is $2,500. The remittance amount is unknown. The interest rate is 5.25 per cent; the number of years is 4; there will be 365 compoundings and 52 deposits each year. Given these values, your computer should produce a remittance amount of

$10.81. The "remittances made at end of period" problem is insignificant here because the periods are only one week long.

Q. Following your son's good example, you decide to save up for a new car of your own. The kind of car you want will cost about $14,000, however. You decide you can set aside $200 a month in a special account that will earn 9 per cent interest, compounded monthly. Who will be able to buy a car first, you or your son?

A. This time the future value is $14,000, the remittance is $200, and the interest rate is 9 per cent. The number of years is unknown. Interest will be compounded and remittances will be made 12 times a year. Your computer should indicate it will take 4.71 years to amass the required sum. Because of the "remittance at end of period" problem, it will actually take one month (.0833 years) less than that if you make your first deposit today rather than a month from now. Either way, your son will have his car before you have yours.

Interest-Rate Iterations

The word *iteration* means the process of repeating something again and again. As mentioned earlier, there is no formula that can directly determine an annuity's unknown interest rate. But *you* can do it, quickly thanks to your computer, by repeatedly calculating the future value of the annuity with different interest rates.

Here's an example. Your life insurance agent offers you a $50,000 life insurance policy with a $1,424 annual premium. If you are still alive 20 years from now, you can cash the policy in at its $50,000 face value. What interest rate does the policy pay provided that you don't die?

Enter $1,424 as the remittance, 20 for the number of years, quarterly compounding, and one remittance per year. Now take a guess at the interest rate. How about 10 per cent? Plug that in, and tell your computer to calculate a future value. It will respond with $85,176.54. Since we know the future value of the transaction is actually $50,000, our interest rate must be too high. Try a lower one—say 3 per cent.

Now the future value comes out as $38,395.70. Too low. But we know for sure the interest rate is somewhere between 3 and 10 per cent. Try 6 per cent. You'll get $53,157.02. Try 5 per cent. You'll get 47,559.10. Now we know the interest rate is between 5 per cent and 6 per cent. By continuing this process, you can determine the transaction's interest rate, 5.45 per cent.

With most spreadsheet programs, you must enter your interest rate guesses by hand and force recalculation. Some spreadsheets will do the iteration for you. Programmers can automate the process with a loop that does the guessing.

Present-Value Calculations

Let's move on now to the calculations for present value annuities. Programmers can use the following algorithms:

```
Where:
    PV = present value
    PMT = remittance amount
    I = annual interest rate as a decimal percentage
    N = number of years
    Q = number of compounding periods per year
    U = number of remittances per year

    I1 = I/Q = interest rate per period
    N1 = N*Q = total number of compounding periods
    Q1 = Q/U = compounding periods per remittance period

    T1 = temporary intermediate variable
    T2 = temporary intermediate variable
    T5 = temporary intermediate variable
    T6 = temporary intermediate variable

T1 = (1+I1)^N1
T2 = (1+I1)^Q1
T5 = (T1-1) / ((T2-1)*T1)

PV = PMT * T5
PMT = PV / T5

T6 = (FV/PMT) * (T1-1)
 N = (-1/Q) * (LOG10(1-T6) / LOG10(1+I1))
    (these logarithms can be either
    common (LOG10) or natural (LOGe))

I, Q, and U cannot be determined by formula
```

Spreadsheet users should make the following changes to the Future Value template. (Make sure you save the Future Value template before making changes!)

- load the <u>Future Value of a Series of Remittances</u> template

    question window
- change title in row 2 to <u>Present Value of a Series of Remittances</u>
    (Future Value = 0)
- in cell A4 enter <u>present</u>

<u>error section</u>
- no changes required

<u>transformation section</u>
- no changes required

<u>calculation section</u>
- edit formula in cell A33 to (A32-1) / (<u>(B32-1)*A32</u>)
- edit formula in cell D33 to @LOG10(1<u>-</u>D32)/@LOG10(1+C27)
- edit formula in cell D35 to <u>-</u>D33/E7

<u>answer window</u>
- in cell A44 enter <u>present</u>

Few modifications, other than labeling changes, are required. The formula in cell A33 must be edited and plus signs must be changed to minus signs in cells D33 and D35.

Present-Value Problems

When you have your template or program ready, save it under a new name and test it with the following problems.

Q. What is the present value of your salary? How much could you borrow if you were willing to turn every paycheck between now and your 65th birthday over to a financial institution? For example, if your salary is $2,000 a month, interest rates are 10 per cent, and today is your 25th birthday, what's the present value of your future salary stream?

A. The present value is unknown. The remittance is $2,000, the interest rate 10 per cent, the number of years 40, the number of compoundings and remittances per year 12. Under these assumptions, your present value is $235,530.82. If interest rates are 12 per cent, however, you're only worth $198,314.37; at 8 per cent you're worth $287,640.84.

Q. You want to borrow $75,000 to buy a home. You can get a 30-year fixed-rate mortgage at 14 per cent interest. What will your monthly payments be? How much will they be if you take a 15-year mortgage instead?

A. The present value is $75,000. The remittance is unknown. The interest rate is 14 per cent, the number of years 30, the number of compoundings and remittances per year 12. Your monthly payment (principal and interest only) will be $888.65. With a 15-year mortgage, the payment would rise about $110, to $998.81.

Q. You are a bank loan officer. A valued customer wants to borrow $10,000 and pay back about $200 a month. The maximum term you are allowed to make is 8 years. Can you make the loan at a 16 per cent interest rate? About how long would it take your customer to pay back the loan? Round the term up to an exact number of years—what will the exact remittance be?

A. The present value is $10,000 and the remittance is $200. The interest rate is 16 per cent. The number of compoundings and remittances per year is 12. The number of years is unknown, until you ask your computer, which should respond 6.91 years. You round that off to 7, enter it as the value for years, and ask what the remittance should be. Your computer responds $198.62.

Q. Your customer from the last question asks you to call her when interest rates drop enough that the loan can be paid off in six years. Where will interest rates be when you make your call?

A. Use $10,000 for the present value, $200 for the remittance, and the same old 12 for the number of compoundings and remittances per year. Leave years as the unknown. You know a 16 per cent interest rate takes about 7 years to pay off, so the required rate must be lower than that. Try 10 per cent. At 10 per cent the loan could be paid off in 5.41 years. Try 12 per cent. Still too low at 5.81 years. Try 13 per cent. That's better—6.03 years.

Just for fun, try changing the remittance to $20 and see what happens. A $20 remittance wouldn't even pay the interest on this loan, much less repay the principal. Notice that the answer cell for years, and only for years, says "error". This is because even an infinite number of $20 remittances could not pay off the loan. Whenever you see a single error in the years cell, it means the structure of your question is faulty—the remittance is not high enough to pay even the interest.

Q. Your company is studying the acquisition of another business. Six years ago, that business obtained a 10-year, $250,000, 10 per cent loan. Records you obtained from the business indicate the loan payment is $9,959.06. Another member of the acquisition team stops by your office to find out how often the payment is made, but you forgot to ask when you obtained the records. Now what?

A. Tell the team member you'll look it up and turn to your computer. Leave the present value as an unknown. Enter $9,959.06 as the remittance, 10 per cent as the interest, 10 as the number of years, and 12 as the number of compoundings and remittances per year. Calculate. Your computer gives a present value for this scenario of $753,613.72—much too high. Try 2 (semi annual) for the number of compoundings and the number of remittances. You get $124,111.90—too low. How about quarterly? Use 4 for the number of compoundings and the number of remittances. Match. Turn to your co-worker and say, "Quarterly."

Amortization Schedules

As mentioned earlier in this chapter, *amortization* is the process of paying off a loan. An amortization schedule shows the balance of the loan after each payment. It also divides each payment into interest and principal, so that you can know, for example, how much of your house payment represents tax-deductible interest expense—a common question at tax time.

Spreadsheet users can do complete or partial amortization tables very easily when they know the remaining balance of a mortgage. And to calculate the remaining balance you just snap and crackle a few keys on your computer.

CALCULATING CURRENT BALANCE

Say that six years ago you bought a house with a $50,000, 30-year, 10 per cent mortgage. Your monthly principal and interest payment is $438.79. What is the current balance of the mortgage?

To solve this problem, make the present value an unknown. Use your $438.79 as the remittance; 10 per cent as the interest; 12 as the number of compounding and remittance periods. Years should *not* be 30, as you might expect, but 30 minus the six years that have passed, or 24. Calculate. The amount still owed on the loan after six years is $47,830.33. If necessary, you can enter partial years with expressions such as *24 + (4/12)*, which represents 24 years and four months.

CALCULATING INTEREST EXPENSE

Creating an amortization schedule for a single year of the mortgage requires three spreadsheet columns. (You should also make *sure* the calculation order is set by rows, as usual.) At the top of the first column, place your mortgage's interest rate divided by 100. At the top of the second column, place the amount of your monthly interest and principal payment.

In the third row of the first column, place the remaining balance of the mortgage. Next to the balance, in the second column, enter *+A3*(A1/12)*. This formula multiplies the loan balance by one-twelfth of its interest rate, thus calculating the amount of interest paid during January. In the third column, enter $+B1-B3$. This subtracts the interest paid from the total remittance, leaving the amount of January's principal payment.

Now, back in the first column, enter $+A3-C3$ in the cell immediately below the January balance cell. This will subtract the January principal payment from the January loan balance, giving a new loan balance for February. Copy or replicate the formulas in A4, B3, and C3 down through 12 spreadsheet rows, and you should have a table that looks like this:

```
          interest rate as decimal fraction
           /   monthly principal and interest payment
          /   /    outstanding balance
         /   /    /   interest paid this month (bal*(i/12))
        /   /    /    /   principal paid this month (pmt−int)
      .10  438.79 /   /    /
                 /   /
      47830.33  398.59  40.20
      47790.13  398.25  40.54
      47749.59  397.91  40.88
      47708.71  397.57  41.22
      47667.49  397.23  41.56
      47625.93  396.88  41.91
      47584.02  396.53  42.26
      47541.77  396.18  42.61
      47499.16  395.83  42.96
      47456.20  395.47  43.32
      47412.87  395.11  43.68
      47369.19  394.74  44.05
```

Now have your spreadsheet add together the 12 interest payments. Your interest expense for the year is $4,760.29. In the next chapter, we'll again use raw spreadsheet power to solve some interest-rate problems that often confound even the experts. But first, make sure you can answer the following questions.

EQUAL REMITTANCES: STUDY QUESTIONS

1. What is an *annuity*? What is *amortization*? What is *iteration*?

2. You have money to invest. What kind of transaction would create a present value annuity? What kind of transaction would create a future value annuity?

3. You need to borrow money. What kind of transaction would create a present value annuity? a future value annuity?

4. You are buying a home that you expect to resell in six years. You need to borrow $60,000. You can get either a 15-year or a 30-year mortgage at 14 per cent. If you take the 15-year mortgage, how much will you still owe when you sell the house? How much will you owe if you take the 30-year mortgage?

   You can afford the payments on the 15-year mortgage. But your real estate agent has suggested you take the 30-year mortgage instead and invest the payment difference in a money market fund that will pay 9.5 per cent. If you apply the future value of the money market fund against the larger balance of the 30-year mortgage, does the 15-year mortgage still have the lower balance? What if you resold the house after four years? After ten years?

5. In July 1984, Venero Pagano won a $20 million jackpot in the New York State lottery. The lottery gave Pagano an initial payment of $952,380 and then invested in securities that would provide him with 20 subsequent annual payments of the same amount. At the time the interest rate on such securites was in the range of 11 to 11.5 per cent. Approximately how much did New York spend on its "$20 million" jackpot?

ON TO REAL LIFE

REAL LIFE: BACKGROUND

There are still some interest-rate problems we can't solve with the templates we've developed so far. These problems involve all sorts of complexities, such as streams of unequal remittances, streams of remittances made irregularly, streams combined with lump sums, and transactions with interest rates that change periodically.

All these kinds of problems can be solved using what we'll call the *goliah* (rhymes with Toledo, Ohiah; see glossary for etymology) method. Before spreadsheet software was developed, the goliah method was nearly impossible to use. This was so because the method involves building a model of the transaction and calculating the interest of each remittance separately, by brute force. With paper and pencil, this takes a massive amount of work. And the potential for small arithmetic errors that make the entire calculation worthless is very great. With spreadsheet software to do the hard work, however, the goliah method comes into its own.

Formulas have been developed to handle things such as annuities with remittances that increase or decrease a set amount or a set percentage. But the average person will run across such problems so rarely that the formulas are more trouble than they're worth. It is much better to teach yourself how to lay out an interest-rate problem on a spreadsheet. Then, no matter what complexities the problem hides, you will be able to arrive at an answer.

The Bigger Template

Before we lay out and solve some specific real-life interest-rate problems, let's stand back a moment and try to see the forest.

As you pass through life, you'll earn *income*. This income consists of paychecks, commissions, royalties, lottery winnings, earned interest, and money found in bathtubs. Likewise, you'll have *expenses*. Expenses represent the cost of food, clothing, shelter, education, travel, lottery tickets, interest paid, and money lost in bathtubs.

Your *wealth* is the extent to which your income has exceeded your expenses. The concept of wealth applies not only to individuals, but to businesses, countries, and even the world as a whole. Income that is "saved" rather than "spent" is retained as *wealth*.

Investing in Assets

At first, it may seem quite easy to tell the difference between money that is *saved* and money that is *spent*. Money you put in a bank account, obviously, is saved. Money you give to the cashier at Zesto Burger is spent. But what about money you use to buy a farm, a printing press, or a sailboat? There is clearly a difference between the money you spend to buy a car and money you spend to buy gasoline. The car can be resold after it has been used, the gasoline cannot. The value of a car you own is part of your wealth. A car has what we'll call an *economic life*.

In the business world, transactions that buy items that have an economic life are called *capital expenses*. Transactions that buy things that are consumed, on the other hand, are called *operating expenses*.

Figuring out whether any particular transaction is an operating expense or a capital expense is sometimes tricky. But that's why we have accountants. Our purpose here is not to learn how to classify expenses, but just to learn to recognize the pattern—when you buy things that have an economic life, the money you spend still counts as *wealth;* when you buy things that are consumed, the money you spend is *spent*.

The things you buy that have an economic life are called *assets*. Some assets, like farm land, have an infinite economic life. Other assets, like printing presses and sailboats, will eventually wear out. As you use these assets, you "spend" them. As the life of an asset passes, its value (and your wealth) decreases. Accountants call this process *depreciation*.

Again, there are many ways to calculate depreciation. Keeping them all straight is what we have accountants for. Right now your job is simply to understand the pattern: the loss that occurs when assets decline in value because of wear and tear is an expense. This expense is called depreciation.

In the business world, capital is usually expended on assets that can create wealth. A printing press, for example, can be used to produce income. Nonetheless, the ability to produce income isn't an essential characteristic of an asset. You may buy a sailboat for personal pleasure only. Such an asset will not *create* wealth, but as long as it has value it will be *part of* your wealth.

Interest on Assets

Your wealth can be placed in investments that earn interest. It can also be placed in assets that earn income. The transactions are the same in terms of their financial implications. As a simple example, imagine you have accumulated enough wealth to buy a parcel of farm land. You rent the farm land to a local farmer in return for cash payments. In this case, the cash represents the "interest" on your investment.

Alternatively, you might use your wealth to buy a print shop. If you managed the print shop yourself, you would pay yourself a salary. But in addition to your salary, the print shop might also make a profit. This profit is your interest on the money you spent to buy the shop in the first place.

If you were an experienced print shop manager and you had enough wealth to buy a shop of your own, you would have two choices. You could invest your wealth elsewhere, say in U.S. government securities, and hire yourself out to manage Joe Smith's print shop. Or, you could invest in your own print shop and manage it yourself.

Let's imagine the government would pay you 10 per cent interest on your investment. But by buying the print shop you could pay yourself the same salary Joe would pay you and still earn 20 per cent on your investment. This would be a financially advantageous situation.

If, on the other hand, the print shop's annual profit after salary was only 5 per cent, you could do better *financially* by investing your money in the government and working for Joe. (There are many nonfinancial reasons why you might or might not want to own your own business. These often outweigh the strictly financial considerations. This book will show you the *financial* implications of your decisions—but don't forget to throw everything else into the scales when you actually weigh a decision.)

Let's assume for the moment that your shop's profits are 10 per cent. At the end of the year, what do you do with your profits? You can spend them on a Caribbean cruise, or you can reinvest them in your business by buying a typesetting machine, by buying a binding machine, or by getting a computer to make your accounting more efficient.

When you spend your profits on a cruise, you are collecting simple interest on your investment. When you reinvest in your business, you are collecting compound interest.

When you reinvest, your business must show greater dollar profits the following year to keep profits at a steady percentage of investment. If, for example, you bought the print shop for $100,000 and made and reinvested a $10,000 profit, then the next year your investment would be $110,000 and you'd have to make $11,000 to keep your profit at 10 per cent of investment.

Thus, while deciding how to reinvest the $10,000 profit, you have to look for investments that will increase the profit potential of your business. If your $10,000 will buy only one new typesetter, or one new binder, or one new computer, you have to decide which of those three investments will have the best return.

This kind of thinking is called *return on investment* analysis, and we'll discuss it further in this chapter's tutorial.

Liabilities

So far our discussion has assumed that you are purchasing assets with wealth you have accumulated. But there is another way—you can borrow the money.

When you borrow money, you create a *liability*. A liability can be thought of as a negative asset. The money you obtain by borrowing isn't income; rather, it's negative wealth.

The difference between the positive wealth represented by your asset and the negative wealth represented by your liability is called *equity*. For example, if you own a herd of cattle worth $88,000 but the cattle were purchased with the help of a $40,000 loan, your equity in the cattle is $48,000.

Borrowing can be very good for you if you can invest the proceeds of a loan in an asset that earns more than what the loan is costing you. But if the loan's interest is higher than the income of your asset, borrowing will destroy you.

Imagine, for example, that you are president of a savings and loan. You borrow money from investors by means of passbook accounts, CDs, and so on. Then you loan this money in the form of home mortgages. As long as the interest you earn on the mortgages is higher than the interest you pay to your depositors, you will have a profitable enterprise.

Many savings and loans today are in severe financial trouble, however, because the mortgages they made in the past earn interest at a *lower* rate than that currently demanded by depositors.

When a *business* asks for a loan, the investor must determine whether the asset the business intends to buy can create wealth fast enough to pay off the loan, to pay the loan's interest, and to make money for the business. If the asset can't accomplish this, the investor shouldn't make the loan.

When an *individual* asks for a loan, the asset that will be purchased is often non-income-producing. A new washing machine or a new car doesn't usually produce income. But financial institutions are willing to make these loans if the individual can earn income elsewhere that will pay off the loan and the loan's interest. In addition, the asset to be purchased can be used as *collateral* for the loan. Collateral is an asset the institution can take if the loan is not repaid.

When the *government* borrows money, the assets that are purchased are almost never income-producing. Sometimes the money isn't even spent on assets, but on operating expenses. But many people are willing to make loans to the government—in fact *eager* to make loans to the government—because, so far, the government is perceived as the most trustworthy of borrowers.

Government's ability to tax the populace and to print money as needed give investors confidence that their investments, somehow or other, will be repaid. Loans to the government are often described as "risk-free."

The Ups and Downs of Interest Rates

Risk is one of several factors that determine the level of interest rate you will earn on your investments and pay on your borrowings. Other factors include the *general level of interest rates,* the *transaction size,* and the *commitment period.*

COMMITMENT PERIOD

Commitment period refers to the term of the transaction—how long it will last. In general, the longer the term, the higher the interest rate. For example, call your favorite financial institution and ask what rates they are paying on certificates of deposit. Most institutions offer CDs in several *maturities,* such as 90 days, one year, 30 months, four years, and so on. You will find that you can earn higher rates by giving up the use of your money for longer periods. Likewise, if you ask for the current rates on 15-year and 30-year home mortgages, you'll usually find that the rate is higher on the longer-term mortgage.

A factor that sometimes affects these relationships is investors' expectations of the future interest-rate level. If investors expect future rates to be lower than today's, they are sometimes willing to lock in what seem to be rates favorable to the borrower. Of course, if the investors' expectations of future rates are borne out, the locked-in rate will in fact be higher than the average short-term rate over the commitment period.

It is possible to invest your money in accounts that have no term whatsoever. Such accounts are called *demand* accounts. You can get your money out of these accounts at any time, on demand. Standard checking and savings accounts are examples of demand accounts.

TRANSACTION SIZE

If you only have $99.95, your investment opportunities are limited. Some financial institutions offer CDs with a $100 minimum deposit, but many others require more—usually $500 or $1,000. If you want to lend money directly to the U.S. government by purchasing one of its financial instruments, you must have about $10,000.

Likewise, if you want to borrow $99.95, your borrowing opportunities are limited. It's quite easy to charge this amount on a credit card, but the interest rate will be much higher than the rate on a car or home loan. In general, the larger the sum you have to invest or want to borrow, the more favorable the interest rate you'll be able to obtain. Small investments earn the lowest rates. Small borrowers pay the highest rates.

The effect of transaction size is much greater when comparing a $100 investment to a $1,000 investment or a $1,000 to a $10,000 investment than when comparing a $10,000 investment to a $100,000 investment. On transactions over $10,000 the size effect nearly disappears.

RISK

Risk increases a transaction's interest rate. The higher the chances that an investment won't be paid back, the higher the interest rate. The U.S. government can borrow money more cheaply than you can because, as already noted, investors have a great deal of confidence that the government will honor its debts.

Deposits in most banks, savings and loans, and credit unions are insured up to $100,000 by agencies of the federal government. Thus, insured deposits in these institutions are also usually considered risk-free.

As an investor, you should be aware that transactions offering high rates have more risk associated with them than transactions with moderate or low rates. High rates are only available when the borrower can't obtain money at lower rates. (If investment professionals think a borrower can't pay off a loan and interest at lower rates, it is all the more unlikely that he or she will be able to do so at higher rates—tread carefully around abnormally high interest rate investments.)

Risk, and associated interest rates, can be lessened in a number of ways. We've already discussed how a borrower can use an asset as collateral. The investor gets a *secured interest* in the asset. If the borrower cannot repay the loan, the investor can claim the asset. If the borrower owes money to a number of investors, the ones with secured interests in the borrower's assets are always paid off—completely if possible—first; unsecured investors are paid last, if ever. Thus, secured loans generally have lower interest rates than unsecured loans.

Risk can also be reduced by means of third-party *guarantees* that a loan will be repaid. The U.S. government guarantees many types of loans. For example, such guarantees are available to qualified students, home buyers, farmers, and small businesses. Sometimes a close relative will guarantee a loan by *cosigning* it. This means the relative signs the loan forms and promises to repay the loan if the borrower doesn't.

GENERAL LEVEL OF INTEREST RATES

The degree to which commitment period, transaction size, and risk affect interest rates is fairly constant. The general level of interest rates, however, is volatile. It changes from day to day and can move several percentage points in a few months.

Interestingly, if you are a very small investor or borrower, you may not be affected by these rate changes. The low rates financial institutions pay on passbook accounts and the high rates they charge on credit card accounts are fairly stable. As you invest or borrow larger sums, however, the rates you deal with will change frequently.

You must be aware of the general level of interest rates if you want to make sound financial decisions. There are many different kinds of rates you can track. One popular one is the *prime rate,* which is the rate the dozen or so largest commercial banks charge big corporations.

Another popular indicator is the rate the U.S. government pays at its weekly Treasury bill auctions. At these auctions the government borrows money by selling 13-week and 26-week Treasury bills to the public. The T-bill rate doesn't make a good indicator, however, because it's a *discount* rate and isn't directly comparable with other rates. We'll discuss the confusion caused by discount rates further in Chapter 6.

Money market funds probably provide the best indicator of the prevailing interest rate for the average investor. These accounts are offered primarily by insurance companies and brokerage firms. A list of these funds and their current rates, which change constantly, is printed weekly in many newspapers. The average rate paid by money market funds makes a good indicator because it is always current; the funds have no commitment period (deposits made to most money market funds are available on demand); the minimum deposit required to open an account with one of the funds is relatively small (usually $500 to $2,500); and the accounts have a very low degree of risk (although they do carry more risk than an insured account or a government security).

Thus, when you wish to evaluate an investment, you can compare the offer with what a money market fund offers. If the offer you're considering includes a commitment period, a large deposit, or a degree of risk, the offer's interest rate should be higher than that of the money market fund. If it isn't, the offer is of questionable value to you.

You Be the Banker

While the rate available from a money market fund may be the best interest-rate indicator for the average investor, it may not the best for you. The best indicator is the rate at which *you can invest your money.* If you run a small business, for example, you may be able to earn far higher returns than a money market fund offers by investing in your business.

Besides knowing the interest rate at which you can invest money, you should also know the rate you're paying on any borrowed money and what it would cost to borrow more. The most important interest-rate indicator to your financial well-being is the difference between the rate you can earn by investing money and the rate you must pay to borrow money.

Most people will find that the rate at which they can borrow money is higher than the rate at which they can earn by investing it. For example, compare today's money market fund rates with today's car loan or home mortgage rates. Yes, friends, what you can earn in this situation is *always* less than what you'll have to pay.

Some people find themselves in special situations, however. Consider anyone who bought and mortgaged a home in the sixties or early seventies. The rates these people are paying on their mortgages are below the rates at which they can now invest money. If someone in this circumstance inherited, won, or found enough money to pay off the mortgage, *it would be a mistake* to do so. Better to invest the money at a higher rate, continue to pay off the loan at the lower rate, and pocket the difference.

Or consider anyone who has found an investment that earns at a higher rate than the prevailing cost of money. A print shop owner, for example, might know that a new typesetting machine will have a rate of return of 20 per cent. If money can be borrowed at 14 per cent, the print shop owner will pocket the 6 per cent difference.

People in these special situations are like bankers. They borrow low and invest high.

Financial Strategy 101

You have income. You have expenses. If your income is greater than what you spend, you have assets. These assets may be as simple as a pocketful of change, as useless as great-grandpa's spats, as exotic as a yacht, as prolific as a warren of rabbits.

You can increase your assets with borrowed money; but when you do, the liability of the borrowed money will offset those assets in an accounting of your wealth (or *net worth*).

If your assets earn at a rate higher than your liabilities, your financial situation is improving. But when your liabilities have the higher rate, your financial situation is worsening.

Whenever you can borrow money for *less* than what you can earn with it, borrow all you can and pay it back as slowly as possible.

But if borrowed money costs *more* than what you can earn with it, borrow as little as necessary and pay it back as fast as possible.

REAL LIFE: SUMMARY

1. *Wealth* is the extent to which a person's lifetime income has exceeded his or her expenses.

2. Wealth is invested in *assets*. Assets can also be purchased with borrowed money, but the borrowing creates a *liability*. Your *equity* in the asset is the value of the asset minus any loans or other liabilities associated with that asset.

3. Some kinds of assets earn interest or other income (bank accounts). Some kinds of assets *depreciate*, or lose value, because of wear and tear (sailboats). Some do both (printing presses), some neither (gold).

4. The interest rates you earn or pay on a transaction are affected by the length of the commitment period of the transaction, the size of the transaction, the degree of risk involved, and the general level of interest rates.

5. To make sound financial decisions, you must be aware of the general level of interest rates. The average rate paid by money market funds is a good index for most individuals.

6. The most important interest-rate indicator for your financial well-being is the difference between the rate *you* can earn by investing money and the rate *you* must pay to borrow money. If the borrowing rate is higher, borrow as little as possible and pay it off as fast as you can. If the earning rate is higher, borrow as much as possible and pay it off as slowly as you can.

REAL LIFE: TUTORIAL

The formulas we've looked at up till now provide quick solutions to standard interest-rate problems. Many real-life problems, however, aren't standard. They involve quantities—interest rates, remittances, or amounts of time—that change over the course of the transaction.

In this tutorial you're going to learn how to solve any kind of interest-rate problem by laying it out with a spreadsheet program. The same kind of thing could be done with a programming language such as BASIC, but it takes longer and it is harder to verify the result. In addition, each problem you encountered would probably require a new program. The real efficiency of programming languages derives from using the software you develop over and over again. If your program is only going to be used once, it is often less time-consuming to forego programming languages such as BASIC completely and solve the problem with pencil and paper.

Until recently, the solutions to these kinds of problems were guessed at, estimated, or left in the great dark void of the unknown. Paper and pencil solutions are so time-consuming—particularly if iteration is involved—that guessing was considered more efficient.

But personal computers and spreadsheets now give all of us the power to peer into the great dark void and pull out accurate solutions to our real-life problems. Here's how.

The Goliah Template

Begin with a clean worksheet. Then:

- set the global column width to 11
- set the calculation order to "rows"
- set calculation to "manual"

Most spreadsheet programs show seven columns on 80-column display when the column width has been set to 11. If yours doesn't, reduce the width to 10, since the template we're developing uses seven columns.

In rows 2 and 3, right justify and enter the following labels:

```
year    period   bgn bal   remit at   int rate   interest   remit at
                           prd strt   /period    amount     prd end
```

In row 5, under "year", put a 1. In the "beginning balance", "remittance at period start", "interest rate/period" and "remittance at period end" columns, put 0s. In the "interest amount" column, put a formula that adds together row 5's "beginning balance" and "remit at period start", then multiplies the sum by "interest rate/period". The VisiCalc-format command for this would be *(C5 +D5)*E5*.

In row 6, enter a formula in the "beginning balance" column that adds together the "beginning balance", the "remittance at period start", the "interest amount", and the "remittance at period end" cells from the previous row. A sample formula would be *@SUM(C5..D5,F5...G5)*.

Next enter a formula that brings the value in the two remittance columns and the interest-rate columns down a row. These formulas would be *+D5*, *+E5*, and *+G5*. Also, copy or replicate the formula in the "interest amount" column to row 6.

Your template should now look like this:

```
year    period   bgn bal   remit at   int rate   interest   remit at
                           prd strt   /period    amount     prd end
 1                            0          0          0          0
                  0           0          0          0          0
```

Now save the goliah template. That's it. Everything else will vary from problem to problem.

YEAR AND PERIOD

As we develop goliah solutions to interest-rate problems, we will use one spreadsheet row for each time period in the problem. The "year" and "period" columns are for numbering these periods. The numbers aren't usually used in any formulas; they're just there to help you keep track of where you are in the spreadsheet.

For example, if you were working on a problem that had quarterly compounding over a five-year period, you would begin by setting up your spreadsheet like this:

year	period	bgn bal	remit at prd strt	int rate /period	interest amount	remit at prd end
1	1	0	0	0	0	0
	2	0	0	0	0	0
	3					
	4					
2	1					
	2					
	3					
	4					
3	1					
	2					
	3					
	4					
4	1					
	2					
	3					
	4					
5	1					
	2					
	3					
	4					

It isn't as difficult to set up these columns as it may as first appear. By using your spreadsheet's replicate or copy command, you can enter numbers very quickly.

For example, begin by entering a 1 in the "period" column next to the 1 already in the "year" column. In the next row, enter a formula that will add 1 to whatever is in the cell immediately above it; for example, $B5+1$. Then copy this formula in the next two cells below that one. This gives you the quarter numbers for the first period. Now replicate the whole block from the 1 in "year" to the 4 in "period" beginning in the next row. Change the new 1 in the "year" column to another $+1$ formula, such as $A5+1$. Now replicate that block once for each additional year you need. If you need lots and lots of years, replicate larger blocks once you have them.

Admittedly, problems involving frequent compounding, and particularly daily compounding, stretch the limits of the goliah method. Few long-term interest rate situations involve daily compounding, however, so this shouldn't be too much of a problem. But if you do run out of spreadsheet rows (or computer memory, another possibility), there is a trick you can use. I'll show you how it works shortly.

BEGINNING BALANCE AND INTEREST AMOUNT

Once you have the year and period columns ready, copy or replicate (relative) the other formulas in row 6 down to the last row you will be using.

It is possible, as you'll see later, to replace some of these formulas with values. However, the cells in the "beginning balance" and "interest amount" columns must always contain the row-6 formulas, never values. Each formula in the "beginning balance" column must refer to cells in the preceeding row. Each formula in the "interest amount" column must refer to cells in its own row. These formulas should never be replaced with anything.

After you have filled in your worksheet with the row-6 formulas, copy the "beginning balance" formula down one additional row. This creates an ending balance (it's the beginning balance for the period after the transaction has ended).

INTEREST RATE/PERIOD

For the goliah template to work correctly, you must enter the interest rate as a *decimal fraction* and as the interest rate *per compounding period*. It may be helpful for you to enter the annual interest rate, using your preferred format, in row 4 and put a formula in row 5's interest-rate cell that will make the necessary adjustments. If you were using four compounding periods per year and standard percentages, for example, you would change the contents of cell E5 to *(E4/4)/100*.

If you prefer dealing with interest rates as decimal fractions rather than as whole percentages, you can leave out the */100* part, but make sure you enter a decimal fraction in row 4. If you are dealing with other compounding periods, say monthly, you would change the *4* in the formula to a *12*.

The formula we have in row 6 of the "interest rate/period" column will display the value from row 5 of that column. When you copy or replicate (relative) the row-6 formula down the worksheet, you cause that same value to appear *in every cell of the column.*

If you happen to be working on a problem that has changing interest rates, you can enter a new interest rate at any point in the column. When you recalculate, the new rate will be used not only in the cell you have entered it in, but also in all following rows. This makes it easy to deal with multirate problems. But make sure any rates you enter by hand are in the correct (decimal fraction, rate per compounding period) format.

REMITTANCES

Our goliah template allows remittances to be made at either the beginning or the end of a period. This makes the template more flexible than the standard formulas, which always assume that remittances occur at the end of the period.

Just as in the "interest rate/period" column, the row-6 formulas cause whatever you enter in row 5's remittance columns to continue down the entire worksheet. On problems with varying remittances, any change you enter will continue in following rows. It is also possible to throw out the row-6 formulas entirely and use others of your own construction. You might do this, for example, if you wanted a stream of remittances to increase or decrease by a set percentage or amount.

YIN AND YANG

When you are working on transactions involving lump sums or future value remittances, all the numbers in the "beginning balance" column and the two remittance columns will be positive. These problems involve amounts left to grow at compound interest—nothing is ever subtracted from the balance.

When you are working on transactions involving the present value of a stream of remittances, however, some numbers will be positive and some negative. For example, on a home loan you might let the outstanding balance be positive and the remittances be negative. You would do this because the remittances must *decrease* the outstanding balance. You could also make the balance negative and the remittances positive. It doesn't make any difference mathematically which is which as long as they are different.

The examples that follow will help you get the hang of all this. If you don't understand this negative-positive stuff, don't worry—yet.

Solving Easy Problems

Now let's take a look at how some problems (ones you've already solved using formulas) should be entered in the goliah worksheet. At the end of Chapter 2, one of the study questions asked:

> What is a $1,000, quarterly compounded investment worth after 5, 10, 15, 20, 25, and 30 years at the following rates of interest: 5 per cent? 7.5 per cent? 10 per cent? 12.5 per cent?

70 Part I   The SCIENCE of Interest and Money

To solve this problem, set up the template for 30 years with 4 periods per year. This will require 120 spreadsheet rows. Replicate the formulas in row 6 as described earlier. In row 5's "beginning balance" column, enter $1,000. The remittance columns should be blank. Enter the first interest rate, 5 per cent, in row 4 of the interest-rate column. The next cell down should divide this number by four quarters, and then by 100. Calculate, and your spreadsheet should look like this:

year	period	bgn bal	remit at prd strt	int rate /period	interest amount	remit at prd end
				5		
1	1	1000.00	0	.0125	12.50	0
	2	1012.50	0	.0125	12.66	0
	3	1025.16	0	.0125	12.81	0
	4	1037.97	0	.0125	12.97	0
2	1	1050.95	0	.0125	13.14	0
	2	1064.08	0	.0125	13.30	0
	3	1077.38	0	.0125	13.47	0
	4	1090.85	0	.0125	13.64	0
3	1	1104.49	0	.0125	13.81	0
	2	1118.29	0	.0125	13.98	0
	3	1132.27	0	.0125	14.15	0
	4	1146.42	0	.0125	14.33	0
4	1	1160.75	0	.0125	14.51	0
	2	1175.26	0	.0125	14.69	0
	3	1189.95	0	.0125	14.87	0
	4	1204.83	0	.0125	15.06	0
5	1	1219.89	0	.0125	15.25	0
	2	1235.14	0	.0125	15.44	0
	3	1250.58	0	.0125	15.63	0
	4	1266.21	0	.0125	15.83	0
6	1	1282.04	0	.0125	16.03	0
	2	1298.06	0	.0125	16.23	0
	3	1314.29	0	.0125	16.43	0
	4	1330.72	0	.0125	16.63	0
7	1	1347.35	0	.0125	16.84	0
	2	1364.19	0	.0125	17.05	0
	3	1381.25	0	.0125	17.27	0
	4	1398.51	0	.0125	17.48	0
8	1	1415.99	0	.0125	17.70	0
	2	1433.69	0	.0125	17.92	0
	3	1451.61	0	.0125	18.15	0
	4	1469.76	0	.0125	18.37	0

Chapter 4   On to Real Life   71

year	period	bgn bal	remit at prd strt	int rate /period	interest amount	remit at prd end
9	1	1488.13	0	.0125	18.60	0
	2	1506.73	0	.0125	18.83	0
	3	1525.57	0	.0125	19.07	0
	4	1544.64	0	.0125	19.31	0
10	1	1563.94	0	.0125	19.55	0
	2	1583.49	0	.0125	19.79	0
...and so on...
	4	3970.53	0	.0125	49.63	0
29	1	4020.16	0	.0125	50.25	0
	2	4070.41	0	.0125	50.88	0
	3	4121.29	0	.0125	51.52	0
	4	4172.81	0	.0125	52.16	0
30	1	4224.97	0	.0125	52.81	0
	2	4277.78	0	.0125	53.47	0
	3	4331.26	0	.0125	54.14	0
	4	4385.40	0	.0125	54.82	0
		4440.21				

You can quickly pick out the results. Look at year 6, period 1, for the value *after* five years. Look at year 11, period 1, for the value after 10 years, and so on. Do your answers agree with what you came up with at the end of Chapter 2? Change the interest rate in row 4 and recalculate to solve the other parts of the problem. You'll notice that it takes a good deal longer for your computer to solve the problem than it did when we were using formulas. This, and the time it takes to set up the problem, are the main drawbacks of the goliah method.

The other math-intensive study question at the end of Chapter 2 went like this:

> In 1876, the U.S. gross national product was about $24 billion (1972 dollars). In 1976 it was about $1,298 billion. What was the average growth rate in the gross national product over the period?

Using the Time Value of a Lump Sum formulas, we were able to solve this problem directly by placing a question mark in the interest-rate cell. With the goliah template, however, we will have to use iteration.

First set up a template for 101 years with one period each. You could enter *1876* for "year" in row 5 if you wanted to. Then enter $24 for the beginning balance and adjust the interest rate, which is equivalent to the growth rate in this kind of problem, and recalculate until the balance for 1976 is $1,298. This is easier to do if you split the screen into two windows so that you can enter the interest rate in the top window and see the answer in the bottom window.

Try to solve the problem without looking at the following screen display or at the answer you obtained when you did the problem in Chapter 2. This will give you a better appreciation for the main drawbacks of the goliah method and may convince you to use the formulas when possible.

Here's what your screen should look like when you have solved the problem:

year	period	bgn bal	remit at prd strt	int rate /period	interest amount	remit at prd end
				4.071		
1876		24	0	.04071	.98	0
1877		25	0	.04071	1.02	0
1878		26	0	.04071	1.06	0
1879		27	0	.04071	1.10	0
1880		28	0	.04071	1.15	0
1881		29	0	.04071	1.19	0
1970		1021	0	.04071	41.58	0
1971		1063	0	.04071	43.27	0
1972		1106	0	.04071	45.04	0
1973		1151	0	.04071	46.87	0
1974		1198	0	.04071	48.78	0
1975		1247	0	.04071	50.76	0
1976		1298	0	.04071	52.83	0

Now let's look at some problems involving remittances. Here's the first math-intensive question from the end of Chapter 3.

The Case of the Agent's Advice

You are buying a home that you expect to resell in six years. You need to borrow $60,000. You can get either a 15-year or a 30-year mortgage at 14 per cent. If you take the 15-year mortgage, how much will you still owe when you sell the house? How much will you owe if you take the 30-year mortgage?

You can afford the payments on the 15-year mortgage. But your real estate agent has suggested you take the 30-year mortgage instead and invest the payment difference in a money market fund that will pay 9.5 per cent. If you apply the future value of the money market fund against the larger balance of the 30-year mortgage, does the 15-year mortgage still have the lower balance? What if you resold the house after four years? After ten years?

The first thing you have to do to solve this problem is figure out what remittance will pay off a 14 per cent loan in 15 years and what remittance will do it in 30 years. This was quite easy to do when we were working with formulas, but now it will require iteration.

That's not the only complexity. Thirty years of monthly payments means we are dealing with 360 periods in this problem. Many spreadsheets don't have that many rows!

WRAP-AROUND PROBLEM SOLVING

We can get around this problem by taking advantage of the fact that spreadsheet programs calculate row-by-row from top to bottom. When the top row is calculated, the bottom row still holds the results of the last calculation. Thus, by referring to the cells at the bottom of the spreadsheet, we can bring those previous results up to the top of the spreadsheet and continue the calculation. Our first recalculation will figure the first 15 years of the problem; the second recalculation will bring the results of the first calculation to the top of the worksheet and figure the second 15 years of the problem.

It's not as complex as it sounds, but it does slow down calculations, since each iteration will involve two complete recalculations. Begin by loading a blank copy of the goliah template. Set up 15 years with 12 periods per year. Copy the row-6 formulas down through the bottom (row 184) as before. Extend the "beginning balance" formula down one extra row, to C185.

Put the problem's present value—$60,000—in cell C4. In cell C5 put a formula that uses the value in C4 when the year in A5 is 1 and the value in C185 when the year is anything else. How about *@IF(A5=1,C4,C185)?* This magic formula will wrap 30 (or more) years of calculations into the template space of 15 years.

Now enter the other row-5 values as before. The "interest rate/period" is *(14/100)/12*. The remittance is unknown. However, it must be at least enough to pay off the monthly interest charge, so begin by "editing" the "interest amount" formula in F5. Don't *actually* edit the formula, just put your cursor on that cell, enter the edit command, and press return to end editing. This will force recalculation—not of the entire worksheet, but of just that one cell. The cell should now display $700. The remittance must be more than that, but, for the 30-year loan at least, not much more. Try starting with a guess of $710. Remember that either the remittance or the beginning balance must be negative.

74 Part I The SCIENCE of Interest and Money

If you make the remittance negative and force calculation, your worksheet will look like this:

year	period	bgn bal	remit at prd strt	int rate /period	interest amount	remit at prd end
		60000				
1	1	60000	0	.0117	700.00	-710.00
	2	59990	0	.0117	699.88	-710.00
	3	59980	0	.0117	699.77	-710.00
	4	59970	0	.0117	699.65	-710.00
	5	59959	0	.0117	699.53	-710.00
	6	59949	0	.0117	699.40	-710.00
	7	54407	0	.0117	634.75	-710.00
	8	54332	0	.0117	633.87	-710.00
	9	54256	0	.0117	632.98	-710.00
	10	54179	0	.0117	632.08	-710.00
	11	54101	0	.0117	631.17	-710.00
	12	54022	0	.0117	630.26	-710.00
16	1	53942				

That takes care of the first 15 years. Now change the "year" in cell A5 to *16* and force calculation a second time. The balance calculated for the end of the 15th year will be brought up to the top of the worksheet by our magic formula in cell C5. After the second calculation, your worksheet should look like this:

year	period	bgn bal	remit at prd strt	int rate /period	interest amount	remit at prd end
		60000				
16	1	53942	0	.0117	629.32	-710.00
	2	53861	0	.0117	628.38	-710.00
	3	53780	0	.0117	627.43	-710.00
	4	53697	0	.0117	626.47	-710.00
	5	53614	0	.0117	625.49	-710.00
	6	53529	0	.0117	624.51	-710.00
	7	8821	0	.0117	102.91	-710.00
	8	8214	0	.0117	95.83	-710.00
	9	7599	0	.0117	88.66	-710.00
	10	6978	0	.0117	81.41	-710.00
	11	6350	0	.0117	74.08	-710.00
	12	5714	0	.0117	66.66	-710.00
31	1	5070				

A monthly remittance of $710 isn't quite high enough. You can tell because there is still a balance of $5,070 left after 30 years. Change the remittance a little and recalculate until you know it to the penny. At that point your worksheet will look like this:

year	period	bgn bal	remit at prd strt	int rate /period	interest amount	remit at prd end
		60000				
16	1	53379	0	.0117	622.75	-710.93
	2	53291	0	.0117	621.72	-710.93
	3	53201	0	.0117	620.68	-710.93
	4	53111	0	.0117	619.63	-710.93
	5	53020	0	.0117	618.56	-710.93
	6	52927	0	.0117	617.49	-710.93
	7	4061	0	.0117	47.38	-710.93
	8	3398	0	.0117	39.64	-710.93
	9	2726	0	.0117	31.81	-710.93
	10	2047	0	.0117	23.88	-710.93
	11	1360	0	.0117	15.87	-710.93
	12	665	0	.0117	7.76	-710.93
31	1	-38				

Note that the final payment is $38 too high, according to the worksheet (actually $38.18 if cents were also displayed). With a real mortgage, the final payment would be reduced by this amount. When you did this problem by formula at the end of Chapter 3, you probably got an answer of $710.92, not $710.93. The difference is caused by rounding error. If you use $710.92, your answer is *closer* to perfect (perfect is about $710.923), but you would still owe $17 at the end of 30 years. Lenders prefer to have the final payment be smaller than normal rather than larger.

At any rate, now we know that the monthly payment required on a $60,000 30-year, 14 per cent mortgage is $710.93, but this is just an intermediate step on our problem-solving adventure. What we're trying to do is compare the balance of this 30-year mortgage after four, six, and ten years with the balance of a 15-year mortgage. Then we want to figure out which is the better deal.

To solve the problem, the important numbers to write down are the monthly remittance and the mortgage balance after four, six, and ten years. You'll have to put a 1 in the year cell and recalculate one more time to see the balances. You should get a monthly remittance of $710.93 and balances of $59,302, $58,777, and $57,168.

Now figure out what remittance is required to pay off the loan in 15 years. When you have iterated that, your worksheet should look like this:

year	period	bgn bal	remit at prd strt	int rate /period	interest amount	remit at prd end
		60000				
1	1	60000	0	.0117	700.00	-799.05
	2	59901	0	.0117	698.84	-799.05
	3	59801	0	.0117	697.68	-799.05
	4	59699	0	.0117	696.49	-799.05
	5	59597	0	.0117	695.30	-799.05
	6	59493	0	.0117	694.09	-799.05
	7	4602	0	.0117	53.68	-799.05
	8	3856	0	.0117	44.99	-799.05
	9	3102	0	.0117	36.19	-799.05
	10	2339	0	.0117	27.29	-799.05
	11	1568	0	.0117	18.29	-799.05
	12	787	0	.0117	9.18	-799.05
16	1	-3				

And the relevant numbers are a monthly remittance of $799.05 and four-, six-, and ten-year balances of $53,675, $48,919, and $34,339.

The difference between the two remittances is $88.12. Now enter *that* amount as a remittance, change the interest to 9.5 per cent *(9.5/12)/100*, and change the beginning balance to 0. Calculate. Now your worksheet shows you the future value of the money in the hypothetical money market fund. Check out the balance after four, six, and ten years. Your worksheet should show $5,121, $8,507, and $17,543.

Subtract these values from the 30-year balances and you'll discover that the 15-year mortgage, under the conditions stated in this problem, is always a better deal. (To make the 30-year mortgage better, the money market fund would have to earn a higher interest rate than the rate on the mortgage.)

The Case of the Low-Cost Lottery

Here's the other math-intensive problem from Chapter 3:

In July 1984, Venero Pagano won a $20 million jackpot in the New York State lottery. The lottery gave Pagano an initial payment of $952,380 and then invested in securities that would provide him with 20 subsequent annual payments of the same amount. At the time, the interest rate on such securities was in the range of 11 to 11.5 per cent. Approximately how much did New York spend on its "$20 million" jackpot?

In this problem we have to figure out what "present value" New York would have to invest at 11 to 11.5 per cent interest to create an annuity that would make 20 annual payments of $952,380.

Load a blank goliah template and put the numbers 1 through 21 in the "year" column. Leave the "period" column blank, since we are dealing with an annual payment. In the "interest rate/period" column, use the midpoint of the interest rate range given, 11.25 per cent. Since we are dealing with annual compounding, the formula for E5 would be simply *11.25/100*.

The "remittance at period end" would be −*952,380*. At 11.25 per cent, New York could earn that much from now to eternity with an initial deposit of $8,465,600 (952,380 / (11.25/100)). Since the annuity can cancel itself out in 20 years, the true deposit will be less than that. Let's start with a wild guess of $7 million. Enter 7,000,000 in the "beginning balance" cell and calculate. Your worksheet should look like this:

year	period	bgn bal	remit at prd strt	int rate /period	interest amount	remit at prd end
1		7000000	0	.1125	787500	-952380
2		6835120	0	.1125	768951	-952380
3		6651691	0	.1125	748315	-952380
4		6447626	0	.1125	725358	-952380
5		6220604	0	.1125	699818	-952380
6		5968042	0	.1125	671405	-952380
15		1946078	0	.1125	218934	-952380
16		1212632	0	.1125	136421	-952380
17		396673	0	.1125	44626	-952380
18		-511081	0	.1125	-57497	-952380
19		-1520958	0	.1125	-171108	-952380
20		-2644445	0	.1125	-297500	-952380
21		-3894325				

So, $7 million isn't quite enough to get us through 20 years. As you can see, we end up almost $4 million short. Try other initial deposits until you narrow the ending balance down to within $10,000 of 0 (greater accuracy is meaningless because of the possible range of interest rates). At that point your worksheet should look something like this:

year	period	bgn bal	remit at prd strt	int rate /period	interest amount	remit at prd end
	1	7462000	0	.1125	839475	-952380
	2	7349095	0	.1125	826773	-952380
	3	7223488	0	.1125	812642	-952380
	4	7083751	0	.1125	796922	-952380
	5	6928293	0	.1125	779433	-952380
	6	6755345	0	.1125	759976	-952380
	15	4001222	0	.1125	450138	-952380
	16	3498980	0	.1125	393635	-952380
	17	2940235	0	.1125	330776	-952380
	18	2318632	0	.1125	260846	-952380
	19	1627098	0	.1125	183048	-952380
	20	857766	0	.1125	96499	-952380
	21	1885				

Thus New York spent about $7,462,000 for the 20-year annuity and about $952,000 for the initial payment to Pagano—a total of less than $8.5 million—on its "$20 million" jackpot.

PERIOD DIFFERENCES

When you solved the lottery problem by formula at the end of Chapter 3, you may have come up with a slightly different answer. Chapter 3's formula makes it easy for you to calculate an annuity having just one remittance per year but more frequent compounding. It would be an unusual security that would pay interest annually. Whatever New York invested its money in probably had semiannual or quarterly compounding. How would you solve this problem with the goliah method assuming quarterly compounding?

The trick here is to use four periods per year for the interest-rate calculations, but only one period per year for the remittance. Get out a clean goliah worksheet and let's walk through the problem.

First, set the sheet up for 20 years, with four periods per year. We'll be guessing at the "beginning balance"; "interest rate/period" must now have a division by 4 inside it because of the quarterly compounding $((11.25/100)/4)$; and "remittance at period end" will be paid only at the end of the fourth period each year. Use an @ IF statement to work out the remittance; for example, @ $IF(B5=4,-952380,0)$, in cell G5.

Copy or replicate the formulas through the bottom row, as usual. When you've finally narrowed down the beginning balance, your worksheet should look something like this:

year	period	bgn bal	remit at prd strt	int rate /period	interest amount	remit at prd end
1	1	7234000	0	.028125	203456	0
	2	7437456	0	.028125	209178	0
	3	7646635	0	.028125	215062	0
	4	7861696	0	.028125	221110	-952380
2	1	7130427	0	.028125	200543	0
	2	7330970	0	.028125	206184	0
	3	1705587	0	.028125	47970	0
	4	1753556	0	.028125	49319	-952380
20	1	850495	0	.028125	23920	0
	2	874415	0	.028125	24593	0
	3	899008	0	.028125	25285	0
	4	924293	0	.028125	25996	-952380
21	1	-2091				

Look at the difference between the two calculations and you'll see that New York probably saved itself nearly $250,000 with quarterly compounding.

Up till now we've been using the goliah template to solve problems that are more easily and quickly solved by formula. We did this to give you a chance to get acquainted with the goliah method on problems you already understood. Now let's look at some problems that are easier to solve with goliahs than with formulas.

The Case of the Balloon Payment

A *balloon payment* is a much larger-than-normal remittance in a stream of remittances. Often, balloon payments are used at the end of a series of remittances that is paying off a loan. Remittances might be $200 a month for four years, for example, with a final balloon of $2,000. Such payments can occur anywhere within a stream, however, and any number of times.

My local bank offers what it calls "Lite Loans." The advertising goes like this:

> We've structured a new type of loan that allows you to purchase a new car and pay back only what the car will depreciate in value plus the

loan interest. This gives you a much lower monthly payment than the conventional 36- or 48-month loan.

	amount financed	Lite Loan 48 month	conventional 48 month
Honda	$10,000	$185.69	$275.78
Olds	12,000	230.70	380.94
BMW	15,500	296.47	427.46

(Payments calculated at 14.5%. No down payment.)

Payments will vary according to the amount financed and the residual value of the car.

At the end of the three- or four-year term, you select one of three options: 1) Pay the final balloon amount and keep the car. 2) Return the vehicle to First Continental Bank. 3) Refinance the final balloon amount.

How much is the final balloon payment on the three Lite Loans the bank cites in this example?

Load a blank goliah template and fix it up for four years with 12 periods each. The "interest rate/period" is *(14.5/100)/12*. Enter the Honda's $10,000 beginning balance and $185.69 payment, calculate, and your worksheet should look like this:

year	period	bgn bal	remit at prd strt	int rate /period	interest amount	remit at prd end
1	1	10000.00	0	.012083333	120.83	-185.69
	2	9935.14	0	.012083333	120.05	-185.69
	3	9869.50	0	.012083333	119.26	-185.69
	4	9803.07	0	.012083333	118.45	-185.69
	5	9735.83	0	.012083333	117.64	-185.69
	6	9667.78	0	.012083333	116.82	-185.69
	7	6478.48	0	.012083333	78.28	-185.69
	8	6371.07	0	.012083333	76.98	-185.69
	9	6262.37	0	.012083333	75.67	-185.69
	10	6152.35	0	.012083333	74.34	-185.69
	11	6041.00	0	.012083333	73.00	-185.69
	12	5928.30	0	.012083333	71.63	-185.69
5	1	5814.25				

Thus the final balloon payment on the Honda would be $5,814.25. According to the terms offered by the bank, you could pay this amount and buy the car, turn the car over to the bank, or take out a new loan for this amount.

Since the bank is willing to take possession of the car after four years, the bank must think the car will be worth at least $5,814.25 at that time—about 58 per cent of the original loan amount. Carry these calculations along and you'll find the bank doesn't think quite as much of BMWs or Oldsmobiles—their balloons are about 54 per cent of the original loan balance.

Just for fun, try out the bank's conventional 48-month payments. Do they pay off the loan as you would expect they would?

The Case of ROI

ROI is business talk for *return on investment*. The word is usually used in the context of capital-expense planning, but there are some other uses as well.

Most companies have more opportunities for investing money than they have money to invest. Thus a system of some kind must be used to pick the investments that offer the greatest potential return.

In many companies, particularly small ones, such decision making is based on gut instinct. In larger companies, however, the managers' guts are a good deal less reliable. Thus big-time managers turn to more empirical data. The real value of this data depends a great deal on the sophistication of the managers involved.

Problems arise because, first of all, the results of any potential investment must be *estimated*. In the absence of the long-sought crystal ball, no living being can accurately predict the future. Assumptions and estimates must be made, and the potential results of the investment must be based on these estimates.

Secondly, some procedure must be used to determine potential return on investment and to sift the better proposals from the others. In many companies, the procedures used are pretty crude. For example, one popular technique is to determine the *payback period* of various investment proposals. This is computed by dividing the investment by the expected return per year. For example, if a $40,000 change in your office environment would eliminate the need for one $15,000-a-year employee, the payback period of the proposal would be 40,000/15,000 or 2.66 years. The problem with this method, and many others like it, is that it doesn't take into account *the time value of money*.

DISCOUNTED CASH FLOW

The *discounted cash flow* method of computing return on investment is the procedure of choice for knowledgeable managers. This method treats the income from an investment as an annuity. By using the formulas presented earlier in this book, and, on more complex proposals, the goliah method, it's possible to calculate the true rate of return on an investment.

The *cash flow* of an investment is the difference between the investment's income and its expenses. Expenses include both operating expenses and capital expenses. Since full capital expenses are included in cash flow, depreciation is ignored.

Cash can flow into or out of an investment. Cash flow is similar to "profit," except that profit calculations disregard all capital expenses except those that seep in via depreciation. Cash flow, on the other hand, ignores depreciation and counts all capital expenses immediately.

Discounted means, as we have learned in previous chapters, that the true value of a cash flow or any other annuity is less than the total amount received, because future remittances are worth less than remittances made today. The calculations for a "discounted cash flow" are exactly the same as those for the present value of an annuity.

The word "discount" is used in three entirely different ways in the context of interest rates. We'll explore the other meanings in Chapter 6. For now, just remember that the usage of "discount" we've just talked about is common but is not the only meaning professionals have for the word.

A NEW PUBLICATION

So now you're the chairman of a big publishing company. Some members of your staff have a proposal for a new magazine. Their cash-flow projections for this publication are in the following table. The cash flow in early years is negative because the publication will be losing money for a few years. They want you to fund that. The large lump sum in the tenth year is their estimation of the publication's value on the open market at that time.

You can invest your company's money elsewhere with similar risk at 19.5 per cent. Assuming you trust your staff's estimates, should you approve start-up of the publication? Here are the cash-flow projections:

year	projected cash flow (million $)	
1	-2.4	
2	-1.8	
3	-.8	
4	0	
5	1	
6	4	
7	6	
8	8	
9	6	
10	25	(publication to be sold in year 10)

To solve this problem, set up a goliah template for 10 years. Since cash flow will occur throughout the year, put half of each year's cash flow in the "remittance at period start" column and half in the "remittance at period end" column. Start off with the alternate-investment interest rate of 19.5 per cent and calculate. Your worksheet should look something like this:

year period	bgn bal	remit at prd strt	int rate /period	interest amount	remit at prd end
			19.5		
1	0	-1.2	.195	-.23	-1.2
2	-2.63	-.9	.195	-.69	-.9
3	-5.12	-.4	.195	-1.08	-.4
4	-7.00	0	.195	-1.37	0
5	-8.37	.5	.195	-1.53	.5
6	-8.90	2	.195	-1.35	2
7	-6.24	3	.195	-.63	3
8	-.88	4	.195	.61	4
9	7.73	3	.195	2.09	3
10	15.83	12.5	.195	5.52	12.5
11	46.35				

This analysis shows that the publication would appear to be a poor investment for many years. By the end of the seventh year, however, the original investment would be nearly paid off at 19.5 per cent interest and additional cash flows would still be forthcoming.

The $46.35 million balance at the end of the 10 years looks real impressive, but doesn't impart any meaningful information. This is the future value of the cash flow. Since the cash flow is a present value annuity, however, we know that the *true* future value should be zero.

You can force the future value to zero by adjusting either the interest rate or the beginning balance.

If you force the future value to zero by adjusting the interest rate, you are calculating what the professionals call the cash flow's *internal rate of return*. This is a true return-on-investment figure—the one Harvard Business School graduates use. After a little iteration, your worksheet should look like this (you can fine tune till the future value is *exactly* zero if you want, but once you know the interest rate to one decimal place, further refinement is pretty meaningless):

year	period	bgn bal	remit at prd strt	int rate /period	interest amount	remit at prd end
				40.4		
	1	0.00	-1.2	.404	-.48	-1.2
	2	-2.88	-.9	.404	-1.53	-.9
	3	-6.21	-.4	.404	-2.67	-.4
	4	-9.69	0	.404	-3.91	0
	5	-13.60	.5	.404	-5.29	.5
	6	-17.89	2	.404	-6.42	2
	7	-20.31	3	.404	-6.99	3
	8	-21.30	4	.404	-6.99	4
	9	-20.30	3	.404	-6.99	3
	10	-21.28	12.5	.404	-3.55	12.5
	11		.17			

An internal rate of return analysis uses a cash flow that includes both negative and positive elements and forces both the present value (beginning balance) and future value (ending balance) to zero. The true ROI of the magazine investment is a little over 40 per cent. Remember, however, that because of the number of years it takes for the investment to pay off its early debts, there is a lot of risk involved. Estimates of what might happen so far into the future are usually not as reliable as shorter-term estimates.

The other way to force the future value of a cash flow to zero is by adjusting the beginning balance while leaving the interest rate at a predetermined figure—19.5 per cent in the foregoing example. The resulting beginning balance is what the professionals call the *net present value* of the cash flow at that interest rate. To determine a net present value, the cash flow itself must include both its negative and positive elements.

Here's an example. A $100,000 30-year home mortgage at 10 per cent has monthly payments of $877.57. The present value of that mortgage at that rate is $100,000. The *net* present value of that mortgage to the lender depends on the rate of interest at which the lender can borrow money. Say the lender can get the $100,000 at 8 per cent. The present value of a 30-year monthly cash flow of $877.57 for 30 years at 8 per cent is $119,598. Thus the *net* present value, to the lender, of $877.57 for 30 years is $19,598 (subtract the $100,000 he has to give you in return for your 30 years of remittances from present value of $119,598). A nice piece of change.

All About @NPV

I'm a little afraid to finish this chapter, because you may get mad. Most spreadsheet programs have at least a few financial functions for calculating things such as present values and interest rates. Lots of the stuff we've done in this and previous chapters would have been a good deal easier had we used these functions.

The reason we didn't is that your *understanding* of how interest rates work would have been less. Now that you have a good understanding of how interest rates work, here's the scoop on spreadsheet financial functions.

Read your manual to discover what financial functions your spreadsheet has. Functions for determining future value, present value, and payments all usually assume a series of *equal* remittances. Most spreadsheets also include a function called @NPV (net present value) that is sort of a mini goliath template. You can use it with cash flows having either equal or unequal remittances. But don't let the name of this functions fool you—you can do more with it than calculate net present value (and you can easily calculate net present value incorrectly if you don't know what you're doing).

The syntax for this function is @NPV*(interest rate per period, range of remittances)*. For example, you could set up the publishing problem on a spreadsheet like this:

```
.404        -2.4
            -1.8
0.00        -.8
              0
              1
              4
              6
              8
              6
             25
```

The column of numbers on the right is the cash flow. The top number on the left is the interest rate per period, *expressed as a decimal fraction*. The lower number on the left is the present value of the cash flow at that interest rate. The formula in this cell is *@NPV(A1,B1...B10)*.

If the cash flow includes only incoming cash, @NPV returns the present value of that cash flow. If the cash flow includes both positive and negative flows, @NPV returns the *net* present value. Force a net present value to zero by adjusting the interest rate and you'll determine the cash flow's internal rate of return.

Two notes of caution about @NPV. Not only must the interest rate be a decimal fraction, it must be the interest rate *per period*. If you use @NPV on problems with several remittances a year, you must adjust the interest rate accordingly. The second thing about @NPV is that, like the earlier formulas we looked at, it assumes that all remittances are made *at the end of the period*.

REAL LIFE: STUDY QUESTIONS

1. What's the difference between *capital expenses* and *operating expenses*? Which of these kinds of expense is *depreciation*? What is a *balloon payment*? Is a *cash flow* an annuity? What's the difference between a *discounted cash flow* and the *present value of an annuity*? What is ROI?

2. What four factors affect the interest rate you'll pay or receive on financial transactions?

3. When is borrowing good for you? When is it bad for you?

4. Using your spreadsheet's @NPV function, calculate how much a bank would loan you for 48 months of $200 payments if the loan was at 14 per cent and had a final balloon payment of $2,000. How much would the balloon payment be if the interest rate was 12 per cent? How much would the interest rate be if the balloon payment was $4,000?

PART II
THE ART OF INTEREST AND MONEY

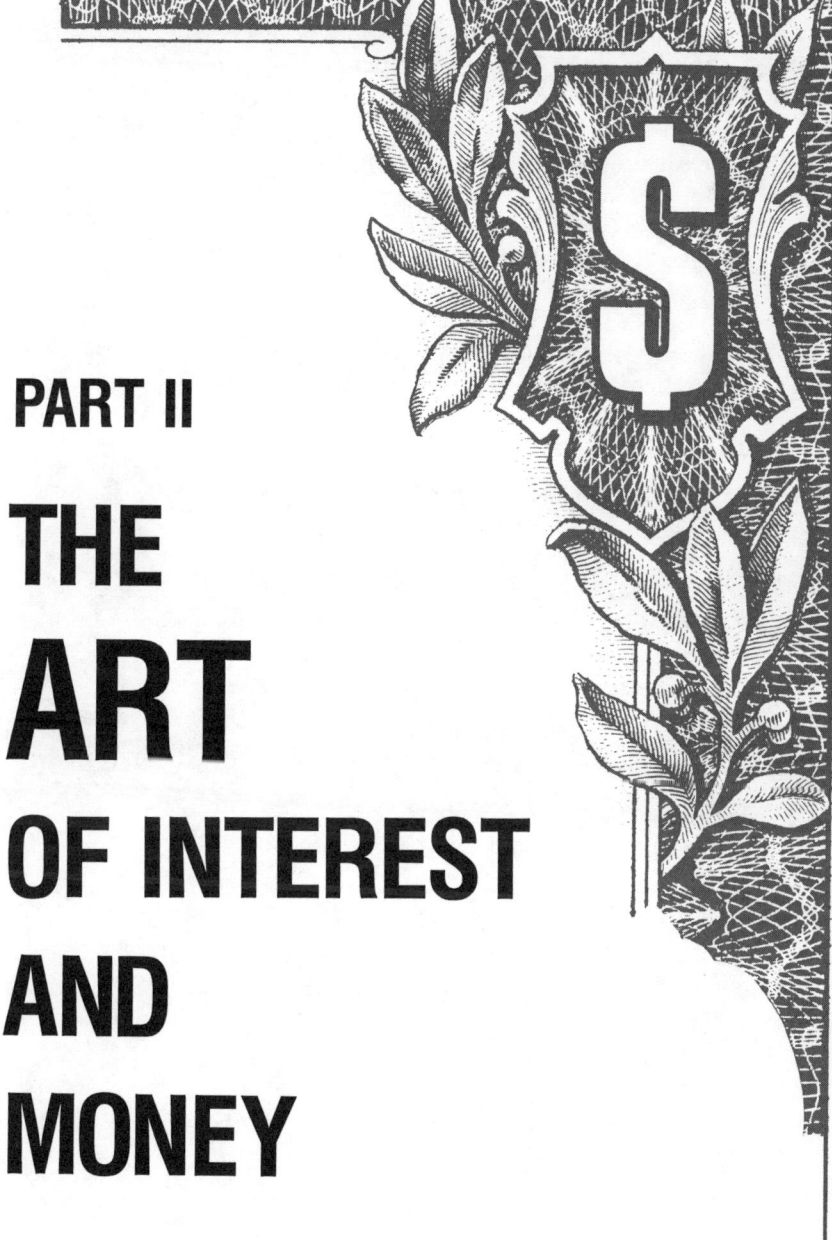

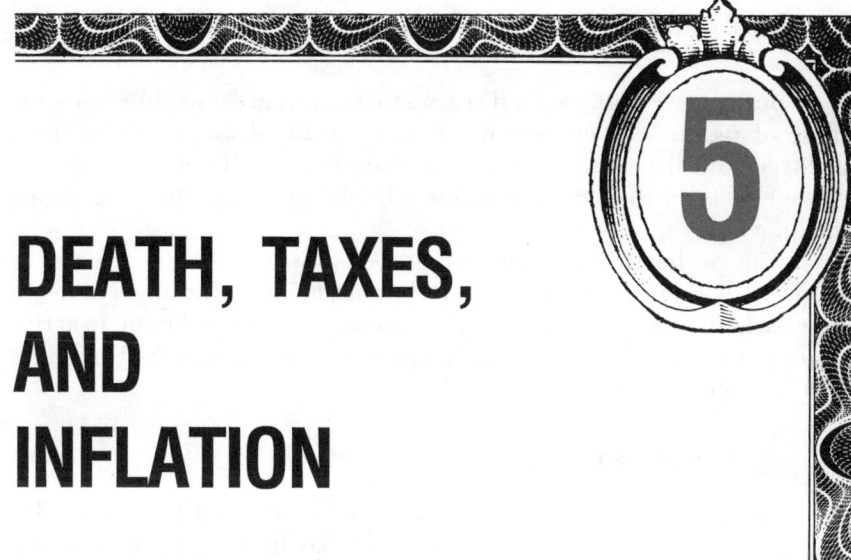

DEATH, TAXES, AND INFLATION

DEATH, TAXES, AND INFLATION: BACKGROUND AND TUTORIAL

Enough mechanics. If you absorbed even half of the material in the first four chapters of this book, you know more about solving interest-rate problems than most bank employees. Often the actual mechanics are not enough, however. You also have to consider the subtleties; you have to add common sense and a knowledge of things beyond the actual financial transaction. The final three chapters of this book will help you understand and recognize these subtleties and show you how to avoid being tricked by the professionals who also understand them.

Death

First let's consider death. Not much fun so far, is it? The main problem with death, as it applies to interest rates, is that "you can't take it with you."

What you leave behind when you die is known as your *estate*. Your estate is the same thing we called "wealth" or "net worth" in Chapter 4— the whole of your possessions, including all assets and all debts. Life insurance representatives will talk to you in hushed tones about the size of your estate, trying to create the impression that it is a great embarrassment not to leave life with lots of wealth (that will be passed out to other people).

But is there really a good reason to die with great wealth? Yes—for those of us unlucky enough to die early in life, leaving behind small children. But if you are older, what's the purpose? If your kids are old enough to fund their own pensions, why should you be funding them? Spend it, I say.

The perfect life for the average person would be to earn lots of money and interest and to spend the last nickel just as the angel of death approached. Since the angel of death cannot be depended upon to arrive at any particular time, however, perfection may be pensions and annuities that last as long as we do.

ACCOUNTING FOR FUN

The great problem with the standard method of accounting for wealth is that funds used for *adventures* are classified as expenses. If you travel to the Taj Mahal, for example, the cost of your trip is deducted from your "wealth." No offsetting asset appears on your books, as might happen if you had spent the money on a pickup truck instead. The spreadsheet summary makes it look as if you are *poorer* for having traveled. But don't let the accounting system make your decisions for you. The Taj Mahal will take your breath away.

Likewise, funds used for *education* disappear from your net worth. But your real net worth as a person will be higher, not lower, when your knowledge and understanding increase. You may even be able to increase your monetary net worth because of what you learn. The "interest" earned by funds spent on education probably exceeds any other investment you can make—but it won't show up on your balance sheet.

One problem with the assets that do show up in the biographies accountants write is that they can be lost. Investments may turn sour. Farm land may erode away. Your partner might go bankrupt. But you'll never lose investments in adventures and education. Not even a bankruptcy court can repossess your journey to the pyramids.

So remember death. Assets are nice, but education and adventures are something not even the angels can take away from you.

LIFE INSURANCE

A great paradox is that the very people who have a good reason to die with a large estate—parents of small children—have the least chance of actually doing so. That's what life insurance is all about. When you buy life insurance, you are betting that you will die before your life's social obligations have been financed. The life insurance company is betting that you won't. Because the life insurance companies have to pay for lots of clerks, computers, and commissioned sales people, the odds will always be in their favor.

Families with two working parents have less need for life insurance than families with only one wage earner. If one parent should die, the other working parent can still supply income.

Unless you find it absolutely impossible to save money without signing pieces of paper that force you to, the best kind of insurance to buy is called *term insurance*. Term insurance is like a straight bet. You put up your money one year at a time and if you die that year the insurance company pays off. At the end of the year neither of you owes the other anything. Most such policies are structured on a multiyear basis, but each year your payment, like the odds of your death, will increase.

Other types of insurance are called *whole life* and *universal life*. These types of insurance have a *cash value*. You make a payment larger than what term insurance costs and the insurance company invests the difference for you. If you don't die, the insurance company still has some of your money and you have good reason to keep the insurance in force—so you can get your money back someday. These types of insurance may be useful, as noted, for people who can't save money any other way. But the price you pay the insurance company for acting as a stern father is usually quite high.

How high? Let's see. Figure out the difference between the price of term insurance and any other policy you are offered. Consider that difference a future value annuity and plug it into our formulas. Use the interest rate you could get elsewhere for the number of years the insurance company wants to control your money. Compare the future value with the cash value the insurance company guarantees. The difference is what it costs you to have the insurance company force you to save money. Payroll deductions into an IRA are usually much cheaper.

When you buy life insurance, there are a couple of things you should consider. The older you are, the more of your social obligations you will have taken care of. It takes more insurance to get a 3-year-old and a 7-year-old through childhood and college than it does to fund a 13-year-old and a 17-year-old. As the years go by, the amount of insurance you need decreases.

In addition, any lump-sum death payment an insurance company makes will have time value. When you remember to consider the interest the lump sum will earn as your children grow, you'll find that the amount of coverage you need is not as large as the insurance company had hoped.

If you have children, the cheapest and most suitable life insurance is not just term insurance but *decreasing* term insurance. With this type of insurance, your annual payment stays the same, but the amount of coverage you have decreases each year. Since with most of us the need for insurance also decreases each year, this is the best solution to the problems generated by dying before your time.

In general, it can be said that people who do buy life insurance usually spend way too much; but people who don't buy any at all don't spend nearly enough.

Taxes

No discussion of interest rates can be complete without a discussion of the effects of taxation. There are lots of different kinds of taxes—sales taxes, excise taxes, property taxes, value-added taxes, and income taxes, among others. However, the tax that most affects interest rates is the income tax. First let's look at how the income tax affects investors. Then we'll look at its effect on borrowers.

THE INCOME TAX AND INVESTORS

Most interest payments are considered taxable income. Consequently, the rate of return your investments earn *after taxes* is less than the quoted or calculated rate. Part of what you earn is lost to taxes. How much you lose depends on what percentage of your income you pay in taxes.

To determine what percentage of income tax you pay, get out your federal and state tax returns for last year. Figure out how much tax you actually paid by adding together taxes withheld from your paycheck, estimated taxes, and any balance you paid when the form was filed. If you got a refund, subtract that amount from the total. If you are self-employed, subtract any "self-employment tax" you paid with your federal return—this is your investment in the social security trust fund and not income tax.

Divide the resulting total by the amount on the line of your federal return labeled "Total income." The decimal fraction that results is the percentage of tax you paid last year. It will be less than 50 per cent.

Say your percentage is 20 per cent and you have money invested at 10 per cent interest. After you pay the taxes on your interest income, you are earning 20 per cent less than before—8 per cent.

YOUR TAX BRACKET

If this much makes you feel depressed, I can probably bring tears to your eyes. Income taxes such as those in the United States are graduated. The percentage of tax you pay on the first $10,000 you earn is lower than the percentage you pay on the second $10,000, and so on.

This is so that people who earn lots of money pay a higher percentage of their incomes to the taxman.

Now imagine that you have $1,000 and you can either spend it or invest it. What you do with the money will not affect your *other* income in any way. Thus, if you do invest the $1,000, the interest earned can be considered the *last* dollars earned during the year. If you think about it this way, the interest isn't taxed at your average rate of 20 per cent, but at the much higher rate paid on the final few dollars you earn.

This rate is called your *marginal tax rate* or your *tax bracket*. Unfortunately, it is somewhat more difficult to determine than the *average tax rate* we just calculated if you don't have the latest tax instructions handy. Sellers of investments take advantage of this by acting as if everyone is in the 50 percent tax bracket. We're not. Take the trouble to figure out which tax bracket you're in.

To do this, look on your federal tax return for the line labeled "Taxable income." The amount on this line will be a good deal less than the "Total income" amount we used earlier. Now look up this amount in the appropriate column of the table known as *Tax Rate Schedule X, Y, Z*. The table for the past year is always in the Form 1040 instruction book. A preliminary table for the current year is published with the IRS forms for estimated taxes. Figure 5.1 shows what it looked like in 1985.

For example, if you and your spouse filed a joint return, you would look up your bracket in Schedule Y—the one for married taxpayers. Find your taxable income in the first two columns of the table. Your tax bracket percentage is given in the third column. If your taxable income for the 1984 tax year was $33,000, your federal tax bracket was 28 per cent. Consequently, a $1,000 10-per cent investment would earn you 7.2 per cent after federal taxes.

Now look up the tax bracket of a couple with a taxable income of $100,000. Notice that it's still only 45 per cent—not the 50 per cent most people expect. In 1984 a married couple had to have a *taxable* (not total) income of more than $162,400 to be in the 50 per cent tax bracket. Precious few people have this problem.

Your state income tax instructions will have a similar table. Add the marginal tax rate shown there to your federal rate. If the state table shows 5 per cent, for example, and the federal table 28 per cent, your true marginal tax rate is 33 per cent.

TAX-FREE INVESTMENTS

In the United States there are certain investments available that are free of income taxes. The low interest rates paid on these kinds of investments usually make them a poor choice for anyone outside the highest

Figure 5.1 Tax Rate Schedule X, Y, Z

1985 Tax Rate Schedules

Caution: Do not use these Tax Rate Schedules to figure your 1984 taxes. Use only to figure your 1985 estimated taxes.

SCHEDULE X — Single Taxpayers

If line 5 is: Over—	but not over—	The tax is:	of the amount over—
$0	$2,390	—0—	
2,390	3,540	-------11%	$2,390
3,540	4,580	$126.50 + 12%	3,540
4,580	6,760	251.30 + 14%	4,580
6,760	8,850	556.50 + 15%	6,760
8,850	11,240	870.00 + 16%	8,850
11,240	13,430	1,252.40 + 18%	11,240
13,430	15,610	1,646.60 + 20%	13,430
15,610	18,940	2,082.60 + 23%	15,610
18,940	24,460	2,848.50 + 26%	18,940
24,460	29,970	4,283.70 + 30%	24,460
29,970	35,490	5,936.70 + 34%	29,970
35,490	43,190	7,813.50 + 38%	35,490
43,190	57,550	10,739.50 + 42%	43,190
57,550	85,130	16,770.70 + 48%	57,550
85,130	......	30,009.10 + 50%	85,130

SCHEDULE Z — Heads of Household

If line 5 is: Over—	but not over—	The tax is:	of the amount over—
$0	$2,390	—0—	
2,390	4,580	-------11%	$2,390
4,580	6,760	$240.90 + 12%	4,580
6,760	9,050	502.50 + 14%	6,760
9,050	12,280	823.10 + 17%	9,050
12,280	15,610	1,372.20 + 18%	12,280
15,610	18,940	1,971.60 + 20%	15,610
18,940	24,460	2,637.60 + 24%	18,940
24,460	29,970	3,962.40 + 28%	24,460
29,970	35,490	5,505.20 + 32%	29,970
35,490	46,520	7,271.60 + 35%	35,490
46,520	63,070	11,132.10 + 42%	46,520
63,070	85,130	18,083.10 + 45%	63,070
85,130	112,720	28,010.10 + 48%	85,130
112,720	......	41,253.30 + 50%	112,720

SCHEDULE Y — Married Taxpayers and Qualifying Widows and Widowers

Married Filing Joint Returns and Qualifying Widows and Widowers

If line 5 is: Over—	but not over—	The tax is:	of the amount over—
$0	$3,540	—0—	
3,540	5,720	-------11%	$3,540
5,720	7,910	$239.80 + 12%	5,720
7,910	12,390	502.60 + 14%	7,910
12,390	16,650	1,129.80 + 16%	12,390
16,650	21,020	1,811.40 + 18%	16,650
21,020	25,600	2,598.00 + 22%	21,020
25,600	31,120	3,605.60 + 25%	25,600
31,120	36,630	4,985.60 + 28%	31,120
36,630	47,670	6,528.40 + 33%	36,630
47,670	62,450	10,171.60 + 38%	47,670
62,450	89,090	15,788.00 + 42%	62,450
89,090	113,860	26,976.80 + 45%	89,090
113,860	169,020	38,123.30 + 49%	113,860
169,020	......	65,151.70 + 50%	169,020

Married Filing Separate Returns

If line 5 is: Over—	but not over—	The tax is:	of the amount over—
$0	$1,770	—0—	
1,770	2,860	-------11%	$1,770
2,860	3,955	$119.90 + 12%	2,860
3,955	6,195	251.30 + 14%	3,955
6,195	8,325	564.90 + 16%	6,195
8,325	10,510	905.70 + 18%	8,325
10,510	12,800	1,299.00 + 22%	10,510
12,800	15,560	1,802.80 + 25%	12,800
15,560	18,315	2,492.80 + 28%	15,560
18,315	23,835	3,264.20 + 33%	18,315
23,835	31,225	5,085.80 + 38%	23,835
31,225	44,545	7,894.00 + 42%	31,225
44,545	56,930	13,488.40 + 45%	44,545
56,930	84,510	19,061.65 + 49%	56,930
84,510	......	32,575.85 + 50%	84,510

tax bracket. Thus, before investing in such securities, calculate your comparable after-tax return on other investments using your true marginal tax rate. Tax-free investments, which are primarily made available by state and local governments, also have a higher degree of risk associated with them than many other investments. Defaults and near-defaults in this kind of security have occurred disturbingly often. For example, if someone tries to sell you a tax-free bond, ask them to tell you about WPPSS (say whoops) bonds.

TAX-SHELTERED INVESTMENTS

Tax-free investments aren't the only way of cutting down on what you pay in taxes. It's also possible to put your money where it will be temporarily sheltered from taxes. You will have to pay taxes on these investments eventually, but you earn interest on "the government's money" in the meantime. Many of these investments are designed so that the taxes you do pay will come due after you retire. At that time you may be in a lower tax bracket.

Some tax shelters are quite complex and depend on loopholes in the tax laws to work. Others, such as Individual Retirement Accounts, are simple and specifically sanctioned by law. Currently, almost everyone is allowed to deposit up to $2,000 per year in an IRA. The amount of the deposit is deducted from your income for the year—you pay no taxes now on the amount deposited. Instead, withdrawals from the IRA are treated as "income"—and taxed—when you begin cashing in the IRA after retirement. In addition to sheltering your deposits, an IRA protects the interest your deposits earn.

However, unless you become disabled, you are not allowed to withdraw money from an IRA until you are 59-1/2. If you withdraw funds before that, a penalty of 10 per cent of the amount withdrawn must be paid, in addition to any income tax due. IRA rules also state that you must begin withdrawing funds before the end of the year in which you reach 70-1/2. If you fail to begin withdrawals by then, you're hit with a 50 per cent excise tax on "excess accumulations."

Another widely used tax shelter results from pension plans that allow employees to make "salary reduction" deposits. You and your employer agree to reduce your salary by 5 per cent, for example, and that amount is deposited into a pension plan for you instead. The amount isn't counted as income to you; thus, you pay no tax on it now. If the W-2 earnings form your employer gives you at the end of the year shows that your "Social Security Wages" are greater than your "Wages," you are probably making deposits to such a plan.

THE INCOME TAX AND BORROWERS

The income tax also affects borrowers but in exactly the opposite direction. Under current law, *interest payments are always tax deductible*. This means that if you are in a 35 per cent tax bracket, every $100 you spend on interest decreases your taxes by $35.

Thus, in the United States at least, the after-tax interest rate you pay depends on your tax bracket. High-bracket individuals, who lose the most on earned interest, gain the most in this case. Someone in the 50-per cent tax bracket can borrow money and effectively get the government to pay half the loan's interest expense.

It is not entirely clear why the U.S. government allows interest expenses to be deductible, while leaving expenses for air conditioners, education, disability insurance, speed boats, and just about everything else you can think of fully taxable.

It is certainly possible to argue that the interest rate deduction is a subsidy the government gives to the nation's financial institutions. If interest wasn't deductible, according to this argument, the demand for loans would fall, cutting into the business of these institutions. On the other hand, it's the borrowers who actually get to deduct the interest expenses—so perhaps the subsidy is meant for them. Only two things are clear: that the government is giving up revenues it could easily collect and that the bigger an investor or borrower you are, the more this arrangement works to your advantage.

There is a movement afoot in the U.S. to simplify the income tax system by throwing out all deductions and making everyone pay tax based on *total* income (rather than *taxable* income, which is total income less all kinds of deductions—some of them obscure and exotic—as is done now). Since this would throw millions of lawyers and tax preparation specialists out of work, it will probably never happen. But many pundits think a modified scheme—one that retains the interest rate deduction, among other plums—might come into being.

Loss of the interest-rate deduction would be a small sacrifice to pay for a true no-deductions tax system. Such a system would help solve the two major problems taxpayers have with today's system—a perception that the system is unfair; and the necessity of keeping extremely detailed records and hiring professional experts to calculate the amount of tax owed.

Inflation

If those of you with money to invest think taxes are bad, wait until you hear about inflation. Inflation, of course, is the term commonly used to describe a general increase in the price of *everything*.

THIRTY YEARS OF FIZZ

When I was a dust-covered boy in the 1950s, our family doctor in Winchester, Kansas, had a 5-cent Coke machine in his waiting room. Last weekend I bought a Coke in Ozawkie, just down the road, for 50 cents. Even after I adjust for the fact that the Ozawkie Coke was twice as big as the older Winchester Coke, the lump sum formulas we studied in Chapter 2 tell me that Coke has increased in price an average of about 5.5 per cent a year over the last 30 years.

The magic of compounding applies to inflation as well as to interest but loses most of its charm.

When you make an investment with the expectation that you will get your money back after a year of collecting interest, you have to consider what the original investment will actually be worth when you cash it in. For example, we know that at 10 per cent interest you'd earn $100 on a one-year $1,000 investment. You'd have $1,100. But if the year's inflation rate was 6 per cent, that $1,100 will buy 6 per cent less than it would have purchased at the beginning of the year. Your $1,100 will actually be worth just 1,034 of the kind of dollars you started with (1,100 * (1 − .06)). Thus, your true earnings, after inflation, aren't $100, but $34—3.4 per cent, not the 10 per cent you thought you'd get.

(Want to add in the effect of taxes? You earned $100 on your $1,000 investment. For our purposes here, imagine that you are in the 40 per cent tax bracket, so you pay $40 of the $100 in taxes. You have $1,060 left before inflation. Reduce that by inflation's 6 per cent toll and you have $996.40; in other words, you lost $3.60 on your 10 per cent investment! Inflation and taxes have a way of taking all the fun out of having money to invest.)

REAL INTEREST RATES

The rate of interest earned after adjusting for inflation is called the *real interest rate*. You can calculate real interest rates and your own real after-tax interest rate with the following formulas:

```
Where:

   I = annual interest rate as a decimal fraction
 INF = annual inflation rate as a decimal fraction
 TAX = your income tax rate as a decimal fraction
   R = real annual interest rate as a decimal fraction
RATS = real, after-tax, annual interest rate as a decimal fraction

    R = ( I          * (1-INF) ) - INF
 RATS = ( I*(1-TAX)) * (1-INF) ) - INF
```

The percentage you use for the TAX variable would usually be your marginal tax rate. However, in some situations, where the interest earned or paid doesn't truly represent the last few dollars of your earnings or expenses, the *average* tax rate we calculated first might be more appropriate.

Like the pain of income taxes, the sting of inflation is felt only by investors. Borrowers feel nothing but joy; they love inflation. Ask people who bought homes in the 50s or 60s with a 30-year mortgage. The dollars they are repaying their loans with are worth far less than the dollars they originally borrowed.

Few people alive today remember it happening, but it is also possible for prices to undergo deflation. This means that the general level of prices *falls*. Unlike inflation, deflation is great for investors and hell for borrowers. Not only do investors earn interest—their dollars are worth more when they cash in their investments. Borrowers, on the other hand, pay interest and must pay back their loans with more valuable dollars. While deflation is something that has not occurred in recent memory, it has occurred often in the course of history.

INFLATION AND DEFLATION SINCE 1800

Figure 5.2 is a graph showing the annual change in the U.S. Bureau of Labor Statistics' Consumer Price Index from 1800 to 1982. In years where the rate is above 0 there was inflation at the indicated rate; where the rate is below 0 there was deflation.

Most episodes of "skyrocketing" inflation, as the reporters like to call it, are associated with wars. Look at the inflation rates for 1812–1814 (War of 1812), 1861–1865 (Civil War—1863's rate of 23 per cent and 1864's rate of 27 per cent pop off the top of the chart); 1914–1919 (World War I); 1941–1945 (World War II); 1950–1953 (Korean War); 1965–1974 (Vietnam War). As you can see from the figure, it is highly unusual for inflation rates to exceed 5 per cent, except during wars. During the half-century between 1865 and 1915, inflation did not exceed 4 per cent even once (1898's 10-week-long Spanish-American War notwithstanding). But the high inflation rates we remember best—those of the late 1970s and early 1980s—don't fit this pattern.

A number of episodes of "dive-bombing" deflation have also occurred over the course of history, but not recently. The last time the U.S. experienced deflation was in 1930–1933—during the Great Depression.

INTEREST RATES SINCE 1857

The most striking feature of the inflation rate is its volatility. Compare Figure 5.2, for example, to Figure 5.3, which shows the average

Figure 5.2   Annual Change in the Consumer Price Index, 1800–1982

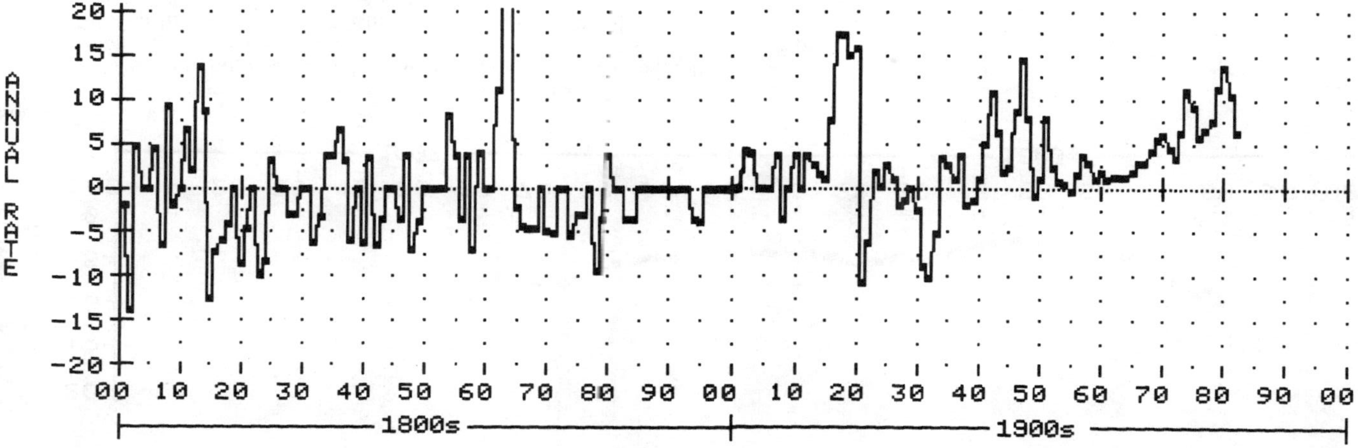

Sources: *Historical Statistics of the United States,
Colonial Times to 1970, Bicentennial Edition, Part 1*
(Washington, D.C., U.S. Bureau of the Census, 1975), pp. 210–211.
Statistical Abstract of the United States: 1984
(Washington, D.C., U.S. Bureau of the Census, 1983), p. 493.

Figure 5.3 Average Annual Interest Rate Available from Selected Corporate Bonds, 1857-1982

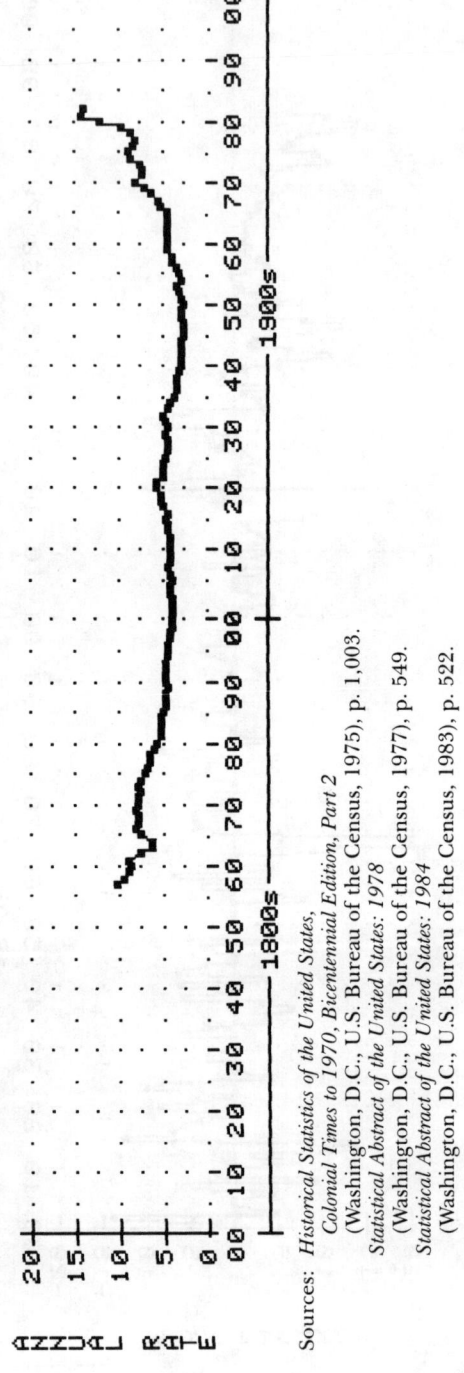

Sources: *Historical Statistics of the United States,*
Colonial Times to 1970, Bicentennial Edition, Part 2
(Washington, D.C., U.S. Bureau of the Census, 1975), p. 1,003.
Statistical Abstract of the United States: 1978
(Washington, D.C., U.S. Bureau of the Census, 1977), p. 549.
Statistical Abstract of the United States: 1984
(Washington, D.C., U.S. Bureau of the Census, 1983), p. 522.

annual interest rate paid by high-quality corporate bonds. From 1857 through 1930, the rates shown are those paid by a selected group of U.S. railroad bonds—no other readily available series of historical interest rates goes back as far as this one. From 1931 to the present, the rates are the average yield of bonds rated Aaa by Moody's Investors Service. For most years, the rates shown in this figure are higher than what an individual would have been able to earn with with money market funds, had they existed (such funds were first offered to the public in 1972).

As you can see, compared to the inflation rate, interest rates have been extremely stable over time. During the 87 years between 1880 and 1967, the highest average rate paid by these bonds was 1920's 5.81 per cent, the lowest 1946's 2.53 per cent. Since 1965, however, interest rates have risen dramatically. In 1981 the average interest rate paid by these bonds was 14.17 per cent—the highest rate of the period.

REAL INTEREST RATES SINCE 1857

But the *real* rate of interest is what investors actually earn and borrowers actually pay. After adjusting Figure 5.4's corporate bond rates for Figure 5.3's inflation rate, you get Figure 5.5—the average real rate of interest available from the group of bonds each year.

In years when the real rate is positive, investors smile and borrowers suffer. In years when the real rate is negative, investors cry and borrowers party.

Again, note how poorly investors did during the Civil War (1864's real rate of −20.76 per cent drops through the bottom of the chart), World War I, and World War II. Borrowers have also suffered greatly at various times, most recently right now.

The 1970s were very hard on investors. During that period an "inflation psychology" developed. People who had money to invest took it out of interest-bearing securities and put it into real estate, gold, stocks and other investments that were expected to inflate in value. Because the real interest rate was negative, many people even borrowed money to finance the purchases. But in the face of the high real-interest rates and low inflation of the early 1980s, those investments don't look so swell anymore.

The real rate of interest shown in Figure 5.4 is based on the Consumer Price Index and on the average interest rate paid by a selected group of corporate bonds. *Your own real rate of interest will be different.* It will depend on the interest rates you can get when you invest or borrow money and on the price changes associated with your assets and expenses. The Consumer Price Index is a good index for individuals, but it is not suitable for many businesses.

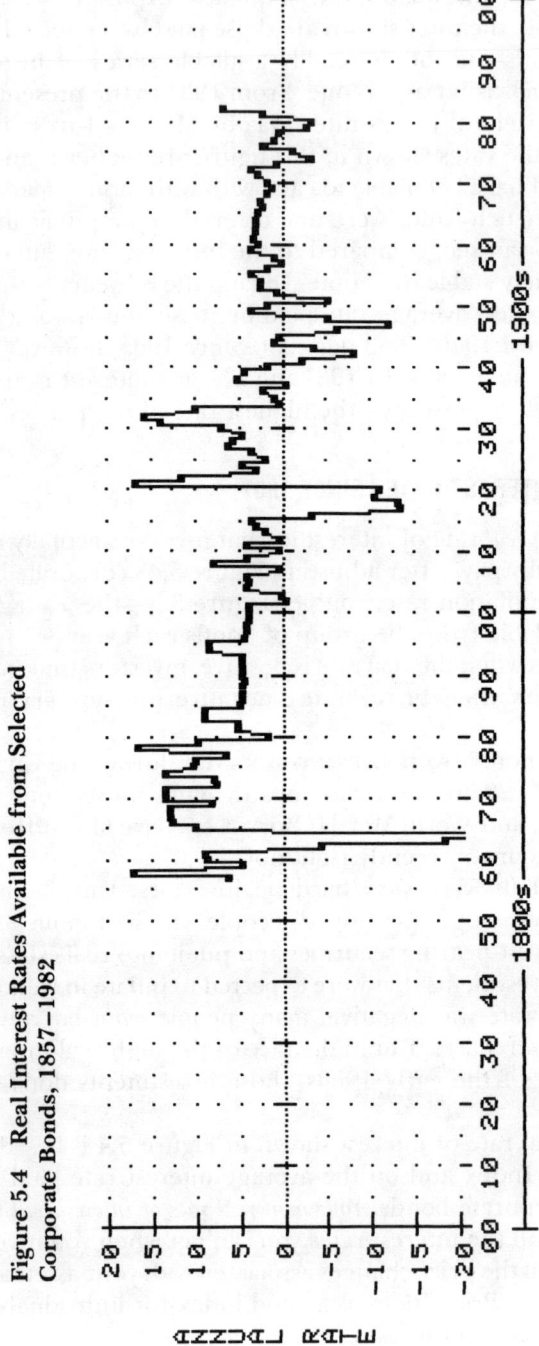

Figure 5.4 Real Interest Rates Available from Selected Corporate Bonds, 1857–1982

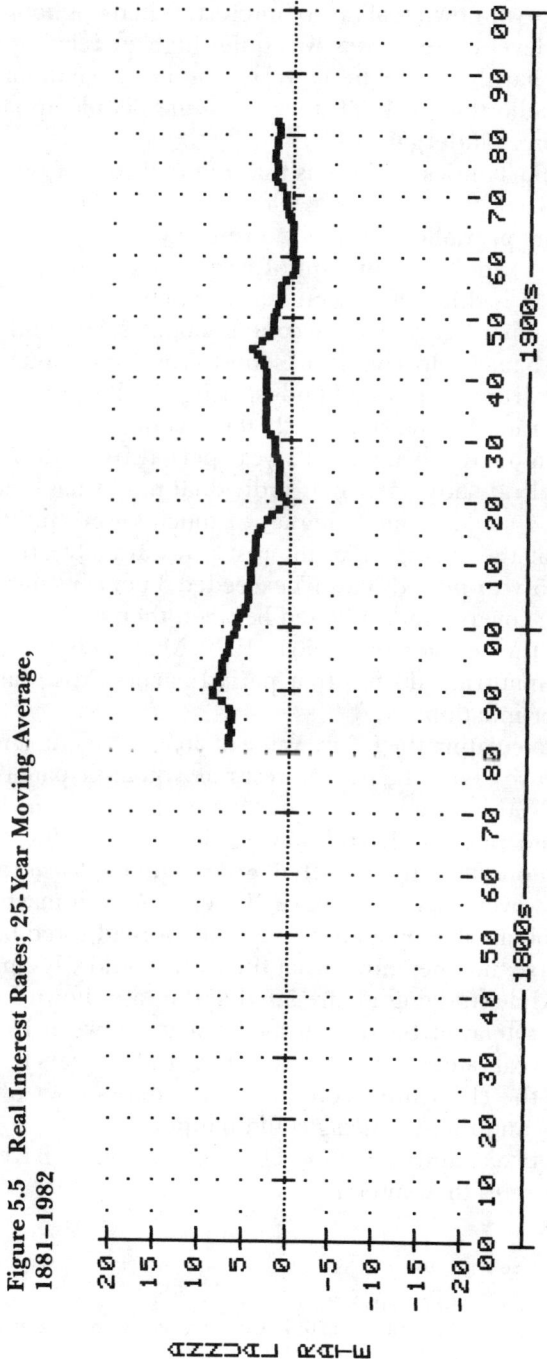

Figure 5.5 Real Interest Rates; 25-Year Moving Average, 1881–1982

Compute your own real rate of interest. When this book was written, in 1984, the level of real rates was quite high in relation to historical rates, but was hardly the "highest level in history," as a national newscaster said on the radio this week. History for some people apparently starts when they enter kindergarten.

The important lesson here is that the real rate of interest you will earn in any particular year *will be more closely related to that year's inflation rate* than to the prevailing level of interest rates.[1]

Because of the great amount of year-to-year variability in the real interest rate, it is difficult to gauge how much long-term investments, such as Individual Retirement Accounts, might earn annually, on average. Figure 5.5 may help a bit. It presents the average annual real interest rate available from corporate bonds during the 25 previous years. For example, the rate shown for 1982, 2.10 per cent, is the average real rate available from bonds during the 25-year period from 1957 to 1982.

The real rate any particular individual might have earned in any 25-year period could be much higher or much lower. But it's instructive to realize that the average real interest rates available from corporate bonds over 25-year periods haven't exceeded 3 per cent since 1946. Even the 1946 rate covers funds invested between then and 1921.

Look at the period from 1956 to 1970. Many people with long-term investments maturing during that period earned less than 1 per cent annually after inflation.

When calculating the future value of an investment, it makes a great deal more sense to use the *real* interest rate you anticipate than the *nominal* rate offered by the investment. Financial institutions hustling IRA accounts often publish charts showing the future value of an IRA at today's high nominal rates (or, often, even higher *fictional* rates). History indicates, however, that rates above 10 per cent, and maybe even 5 per cent, are unobtainable on a long-term, inflation-adjusted basis.

Of course, no one knows what the future holds. It's important that you realize while studying Figure 5.5 that the rate shown for 1982 is the average real rate available during the 25 years between 1957 and 1982. The average real rate available between now and 25 years from now won't show up on the chart until 2008 or later. There's a lot of blank space between now and then; *anything* could happen.

Death, taxes, and inflation. These three things have more to do with interest rates than interest rates.

---

1. The real-interest-rate data shown in Figure 5.4 correlates with the interest-rate data in Figure 5.2 at only R = .20; but it correlates with the inflation-rate data in Figure 5.3 at a very strong R = −.94.

DEATH, TAXES, AND INFLATION: STUDY QUESTIONS

1. What is your *estate*? What is *decreasing term insurance*?

2. What is the difference between an *average* tax rate and a *marginal* tax rate? Which one is equivalent to your *tax bracket*?

3. How can you legally escape taxes on the interest you earn? How can you legally delay taxes?

4. How does inflation affect the value of your investments and your borrowings? How do borrowers feel about taxes and inflation? How do investors feel about them?

LOANS AND MORTGAGES

LOANS AND MORTGAGES: BACKGROUND AND TUTORIAL

The rules that apply to consumer loans for such things as appliances, cars, and credit card purchases are somewhat different from the rules that apply to large real estate and commercial loans. In this chapter we'll look at both sets of rules, beginning with those for consumer loans.

Consumer Loans

In the 1970s the U.S. Federal Reserve promulgated Regulation Z, better known as the *Truth-in-Lending* law. This regulation outlawed a number of unscrupulous methods of charging interest on consumer loans. The law provides that borrowers must be told how much a loan will cost in terms of a true, effective annual interest rate. This rate is called the *APR*, or annual percentage rate, and it's the rate we've been studying in this book.

Before Truth-in-Lending, some lenders used methods of calculating interest that led many people to believe they were paying a lot less for the use of money than they really were. These methods were called the *discount* method and the *add-on* method.

THE DISCOUNT METHOD

With the discount method the interest to be paid is deducted from the face value of the loan before the loan is made. As you know, if you borrow $1,000 for one year at 10 per cent, the interest is supposed to be $100. But under the discount method, this would be deducted from the $1,000 *before* you received the loan. Thus you would actually receive only $900. When you repaid the full $1,000 a year later, you would be repaying a $900 loan and $100 interest—a true interest rate of 11.1 per cent, not 10 per cent.

Although the discount method can no longer be used on consumer loans, it is by no means defunct. Unfortunately, the Federal Reserve has not passed complementary "Truth-in-Investing" laws. Perhaps this is because the biggest user of discount rates is now the U.S. Treasury itself. Every week the Treasury borrows millions of dollars by selling *Treasury bills*, which are quoted in discount rates. The effect is to make government borrowings appear cheaper than they actually are. We'll look at T-bills further in the next chapter.

Discount has two other unrelated meanings in the world of interest rates. Many newspapers carry an interest rate called the *discount rate* on their financial pages. This rate is how much the Federal Reserve charges banks for loans. It is of great interest to bankers and economists and means nearly nothing to the rest of us. Just don't get it confused with something important.

The other meaning of discount was used in Chapter 4. Many people call the interest rate at which the present value of a future cash flow is calculated the *discount rate* of the cash flow. This can be very confusing—remember that in cash flow references the word has nothing to do with the discount method of calculating interest.

In summary, with the discount method the interest amount is deducted from the face value of the loan when the loan is made; the loan is repaid at its face value. A discount interest quote is always lower than the true interest rate of the loan.

ADD-ON INTEREST

Unlike the discount method, the add-on method is no longer a major part of the financial scene. Consumers can rejoice—lenders who used this method were about as ethical as train robbers. Under the add-on method, you borrow $1,000 at 10 per cent for a year. The lender calculates the interest as $100 and adds it to the face value of the loan. Then the lender divides the $1,100 by 12 months and asks you to make monthly payments of $91.67.

The fallacy here is that you don't owe $100 in interest because you don't have the full $1,000 borrowed for the whole year. Your average loan over the year, in fact, is about half that. If you use our Present Value of a Series of Remittances formulas and iteration, you'll find that the true interest rate on a loan of $1,000 with monthly payments of $91.67 is about 18 per cent, not 10 per cent.

Of course, few loan officers used the add-on rate all by itself. Most combined it with the discount method as well. Thus you would go in to borrow $1,000 at 10 per cent. The lender would very nicely point out that to get $1,000 you actually have to borrow $1,111.11. The interest for the year would be 10 per cent of that, $111.11. Divide $1,111.11 by 12 to arrive at a monthly payment of $92.60. The true interest rate on the loan would now be about a quarter of a percentage point less than 20 per cent—double the 10 per cent rate the lender quoted for the loan!

BORROWER BEWARE

Although the discount and add-on methods of computing interest are now rarely used for consumer loans in the United States, the lifeblood of many companies is still getting you to pay them interest.

Consider the couple who bought a new car from a reputable dealer. They traded in their old car and intended to pay cash for the balance, which was about $5,000. But the dealer presented them with a clever offer. Instead of giving the cash to him, he said, they should invest it for three years at the then-going-rate of 8 per cent. To pay for the car they should take out a 12 per cent loan from him. They would actually earn more in interest than they would spend, the dealer said, because the $5,000 investment would grow while the loan would get smaller every month.

They calculated the interest they would earn on their investment as $1,341.21; their interest expense on the car loan would be only $978.58. It appeared the couple would be $362.63 richer by taking out the car loan. There was only one problem—it is mathematically impossible to make money when you are borrowing at a higher interest rate than you are investing at.

Although the dealer's offer looks like a good deal, it's robbery. The two situations are unequal. On the one hand, you would pay $5,000 cash for the car. This involves a single $5,000 payment. On the other hand, you would put $5,000 in the bank and make a $166.07 payment every month for three years. This involves a total of $10,978.52 in payments.

With the dealer's offer, at the end of the three years the couple would have a car with no obligation and $6,341.21 in the bank. The true equivalent to the dealer's offer would be to pay cash for the car and put $166.07 in the bank each month for three years. If the couple did this, at the end of the three years they'd have a car with no obligation and $6,731.74 in the bank. The dealer's offer was the ethical equivalent of stealing the difference between $6,731.74 and $6,341.21—nearly $400—from his customers. And offers like this one are made to unsuspecting consumers *every day*.

Money merchants can create all kinds of confusing situations that appear to offer value. Borrowing money is not as simple as buying groceries. Be careful.

CREDIT CARDS

Usually the highest rate of interest you'll ever pay will be on credit card purchases. Before the Truth-in-Lending law, many firms offered charge accounts with what appeared to be very favorable interest rates. What the lenders didn't explain was that those were *monthly*, not annual rates.

Most states have laws that limit the rate of interest that can be charged on consumer loans. Many states have a two-tier law, with one rate for amounts under $1,000 or some other figure, and a second, lower rate for higher amounts. Credit card companies charge the maximum rates allowed by law in most states.

For many years most credit card companies charged no interest on accounts that were paid in full each month. Many consumers took advantage of this. Charging a hefty purchase to a credit card meant that payment could be delayed—interest free—for four to eight weeks and sometimes more, depending on how quickly the item appeared on the credit card company's monthly bill. Most companies have modified this practice and now get their high rates from just about everybody.

And, in case you didn't know it, merchants who accept credit cards must also pay the card companies fees equal to 1 to 5 per cent of what you spend. If you paid all bills within two months of purchase, these fees alone would provide the credit card company with 6 to 30 per cent annual interest on the money they're loaning you.

The two major credit card companies, MasterCard and Visa, allow you to walk into almost any bank and buy some cash on credit. Unlike with merchandise purchases, however, interest on cash withdrawals begins accruing immediately and continues through the day your payment is received. This is a very expensive way to get cash.

Credit cards do grease the wheels of commerce—the U.S. economy could probably not exist as we know it today without them. Credit cards provide merchants with a security only cash could provide before; and they allow consumers to make transactions without carrying around a lot of money. Consumers who actually use credit cards to obtain credit, however, are getting beer at champagne prices.

PROTECTING YOUR CARDS AND YOUR LIFE

The churls who used to trick people by pretending monthly rates were annual must have moved on after Truth-in-Lending to the credit card protection industry. These folks charge you an annual fee in return for promising to pick up the tab if your credit cards should be lost or stolen and used by someone else.

What they don't tell you is that the *maximum* amount you would owe if your credit cards were stolen is $50 per card. And if you notify the credit card company that a card has been lost or stolen before somebody uses it, *you owe nothing*. Credit card protection may be a good deal for people who carry a pocketful of credit cards. Otherwise, the fees are exceedingly high. Multiply the average risk involved ($25 times the number of cards you have) by the odds that your cards will walk off someday (1/15? 1/100?) and you'll have a reasonable one-time fee. Typical fees, however, are 10 to 100 times that.

The Truth-in-Lending law provides that everything you are required to pay for a consumer loan must be included in the quoted interest rate. Before Truth-in-Lending, many institutions required borrowers to pay various kinds of fees in addition to interest. Institutions can still charge these fees if they like, but the cost must now be included in the quoted interest rate.

Before Truth-in-Lending a very popular fee on many loans was for *credit life insurance*. This kind of insurance pays off the principal of the loan and all interest due if the borrower dies or is disabled. Nowadays, if an institution *requires* such insurance as a condition for a consumer loan, or charges any other mandatory fee, the cost must be included in the interest rate. Thus have most such requirements mysteriously vanished.

But expect your lender to put pressure on you to buy *optional* credit life insurance. A major bank in Kansas City, for example, occasionally includes a flyer with its credit card bills, the outside of which reads, "IMPORTANT: Please complete and return the enclosed receipt along with your monthly payment." The flyer is not a "receipt" by any stretch of the imagination, but an application for credit life insurance. The cost is 36 cents per month per $100 of outstanding balance. This is equivalent to an additional 4.32 per cent interest on top of interest rates already at the maximum allowed by state law. But since the insurance is optional, its cost doesn't have to be quoted as part of the bank's APR.

If your circumstances indicate you should have credit life insurance, you will always be able to get it at a better price by adding the coverage onto any existing life insurance policy you already have. Credit life insurance is priced in terms of the amount being financed and doesn't take into consideration the health of the borrower, as regular life insurance does. Thus, younger purchasers subsidize older ones. Credit life insurance is a great deal for people with terminal illnesses. Unless you are in that category, see your insurance agent, not your lender, for the coverage you need.

Commercial Loans and Real Estate Mortgages

While Truth-in-Lending provides relatively small borrowers with some protection from unscrupulous practices, it doesn't do nearly as much for larger borrowers. Neither commercial loans nor home mortgages are controlled by rules as stringent as those for small, consumer loans.

Fees of various types, going by many different names, are *frequently* charged in association with these larger loans. These fees always have the effect of raising the true interest rate the borrower is paying.

The fees are sometimes called "origination fees," sometimes "buy-downs," sometimes "points." Sometimes the true interest rate is raised by means other than fees, as with "offsetting balances." These techniques go by other names in some states, but they all work basically the same way—they lower the true present value of the transaction. Interest is calculated using an inflated present value.

Since origination fees are the simplest of these techniques to understand, let's look at them first.

ORIGINATION FEES

Origination fees are charged as a flat percentage of the amount borrowed and are usually presented to the borrower as the "cost of making the loan." However, the lender's cost doesn't go up as the face value of the loan does. A lender charging a 2 per cent origination fee would get $1,000 from a $50,000 loan and $1,200 on a $60,000 loan, but the "cost" of making each loan in terms of employee time and paperwork would be exactly the same.

Origination fees actually provide lenders with a method of raising their *true* interest rate without raising their *quoted* interest rate. If you are required to pay $1,500 to borrow $50,000, what you are really doing is borrowing $48,500. The interest you pay, however, will be based on the $50,000 figure.

To calculate the true interest rate of a loan with an origination fee, use the face value of the loan and the quoted interest rate to determine the loan's periodic payment. Then use that payment and recalculate at different interest rates until the loan's present value equals what you actually get—the face value minus origination fees.

For example, a $50,000 30-year home loan with a 12 per cent interest rate and 2 per origination fee would have a monthly payment of $514.31. However, you don't actually clear $50,000 from the lender, but only $49,000 (the lender gives you a check for $50,000 and you give the lender a check for $1,000). A $49,000 30-year loan with a monthly payment of $514.31 carries an interest rate of about 12.3 per cent.

The effect is magnified on shorter-term loans. If the same loan was for 10 years, the true interest rate would be about 12.5 per cent; 5 years, about 12.9 per cent. But if the loan was for just 1 year, the true rate would shoot up to about 15.9 per cent. If you borrowed money for 6 months and made a single lump sum payment at the end of the term, a 2 per cent origination fee would add *more than 4 percentage points* to the interest rate of the loan. Short-term borrowers should make every effort to wiggle free of origination fees.

OFFSETTING BALANCES

Another method used by lenders to increase the true rate of a loan is typically used by banks against their commercial customers. The method requires the loan customer to keep a portion of the loan on deposit in the bank. In truth, this "offsetting balance" reduces the present value of the loan just as surely as if the customer had never gotten it. However, the customer must pay interest on the face value of the loan, and thus pays a higher true rate than the loan agreement indicates.

BUY-DOWNS

"Buy-downs" are similar to origination fees. Lenders first establish the interest rate at which they are willing to lend money. If this rate is higher than borrowers are willing to pay, the lender magnanimously offers to lower the rates if the borrower agrees to pay, in advance, buy-down fees.

But the lenders are charlatans. The true interest rate of the loan will change very little if at all. During the summer of 1984 one Kansas City lender was offering 30-year fixed-rate home mortgages at 13.5 per cent with a 4.5 per cent buy-down; 13.75 per cent with a 3 per cent buy-down; and 14 per cent with a 2 per cent buy-down. All three loans carried an additional 1 per cent origination fee.

To calculate the true interest rate on these mortgages, use the Present Value of a Series of Remittances formulas. First calculate what a monthly payment would be at the quoted interest rate and then calculate the true interest rate based on that monthly payment and the true present value of the loan.

Any present value can be used to calculate the true interest; the calculation is independent of any specific value. $10,000 makes a good round number. First use $10,000 for the present value and 13.5 per cent as the interest rate. This makes the loan's monthly payment $114.54. The true present value of the loan, however, isn't $10,000, but $10,000 minus the 4.5 per cent buy-down and the 1 per cent origination fee—$9,450. By trying out various interest rates with a monthly payment of $114.54, we can eventually find one that gives us a present value of about $9,450. It's 14.34 per cent. By following the same procedure, you'll find the true interest rate of the "13.75" per cent offer is about 14.36 per cent; and of the "14" per cent offer about 14.46 per cent. As you can see, the true rates of the three offers differ very little.

The *monthly payments* of the three offers differ very little as well, unless a lender uses a buy-down to get you to borrow less. For example, if you have $5,000 in your money market account and want to borrow $50,000, a lender might talk you into spending your $5,000 on a buy-down that appears to have a lower monthly payment. However, the payment will be very close to what you would have paid had you borrowed $45,000, without a buy-down, to begin with.

One possible advantage of a buy-down on a home mortgage is that, under certain stringent conditions, the IRS will consider the buy-down fee as tax-deductible prepaid interest for the year the home is purchased. In all other situations, however, the IRS requires that the loan's interest expenses be calculated using the true present value and true interest rate of the loan.

For example, imagine a $100,000, 10-year, 12 per cent loan with an 8 per cent buy-down. This is how the loan would be legally described in written agreements between lender and borrower. For tax purposes, however, the borrower could not deduct the $8,000 buy-down fee as interest. Instead, the borrower would need to deduct the interest amounts shown on an amortization schedule fitting a $92,000, 14.11 per cent loan—which is, in fact, what this loan is—rather than a schedule for a $100,000, 12 per cent loan. If the borrower failed to use the correct amortization schedule, his or her interest deductions would be considerably *less than* what the IRS would have allowed. Thus, for unsophisticated borrowers, a buy-down will often end up costing a lot more, after taxes, than a loan quoted at the true interest rate (which, incidentally, the borrower thought was too expensive!)

The tax consequences of buy-downs also apply to loan origination fees (if you can convince the IRS the fee is *only* for the use of money), although the "interest expenses" your lender provides at year end for tax purposes don't reflect this. It's just one more hidden loophole that only the big-boys with expensive tax lawyers (and the readers of this book) are able to take advantage of.

POINTS

Points work exactly like buy-downs. A single point is the same thing as a 1 per cent buy-down. The only difference between the two is that sometimes, with home mortgages, the *seller* of the home will pay the points on the *buyer's* mortgage. If the buyer can use points to extract an especially good deal out of the seller, the points may, in fact, reduce the interest level of the buyer's mortgage. In most situations, however, sellers refuse to lower the price of a home as much when points are involved as they might on point-less transactions. Thus the sellers may officially pay the points, but the price comes out of the skin of the buyers.

One slight difference between points and other types of fees is that when a home's seller pays the points on a buyer's mortgage, the IRS doesn't consider the money to be interest and no one gets to take a deduction.

Points are usually associated with mortgages guaranteed by the Veteran's Administration or the Federal Housing Administration. These loans are supposed to carry a lower rate because they present very little risk to the lender. The federal agencies stipulate what the maximum rate of these loans can be. Lenders are allowed to charge points, however, and thus can slide around the "maximum" rate with little effort.

PREPAYMENT PENALTIES

Nonetheless, federally guaranteed mortgages are usually a very good deal. Unfortunately, not everyone can qualify for one. Although lenders can get around the maximum interest-rate provisions of these mortgages, there are several other provisions they have to abide. One is that such mortgages can't have any prepayment penalties. A borrower is allowed to pay off the balance of the mortgage at any time.

With many other loans and mortgages, a prepayment penalty is stipulated in the contract and imposed if the borrower wants to pay off early. As it happens, almost all home mortgages are paid off early—almost no one lives in the same house for the full term of a 30-year mortgage. Statistics indicate the average U.S. family moves every six years.

Consequently, lenders *expect* to collect prepayment penalties if they can get them in a home mortgage contract. These penalties are nothing but another hidden method of raising the true interest rate of the mortgage without raising the quoted rate. Since many lenders offer mortgages without prepayment penalties, borrowers should avoid lenders who insist on them.

While you may avoid the prepayment penalty actually labeled as such, you also need to be aware that buy-downs and origination fees have their own "built-in" prepayment penalties. The buy-downs we've looked at, for example, offer about the same *true* interest rate as a standard mortgage if both are paid off on schedule. If the mortgage is paid off early, however, the true interest rate of the standard mortgage will stay the same, while the true interest rate of the mortgage involving heavy up-front fees will jump.

For example, let's re-examine the 30-year 13.5 per cent mortgage with 4.5 per cent worth of up-front fees that we looked at earlier. The true interest rate of this mortgage, *if it is not paid off early*, is 14.34 per cent. But suppose the mortgage is paid off after three years.

First use our present-value formulas to determine the outstanding balance of this mortgage after three years. Enter the $114.54 we found previously as the remittance, 13.5 as the interest rate, and 27 (30−3) as the number of years. The balance after three years will be $9,909.92. Next get out a goliah template and lay out three years of monthly periods. Enter $10,000 as the beginning balance; −4.5 per cent of that ($−450), representing the buy-down and origination fees, as a remittance at period start; and −$114.54, representing the monthly payment, as a remittance at period end.

Copy or replicate the formulas through the three-year period (put a 0 in below the −450, since the buy-down and fees are paid only once), then adjust the interest rate until you have a balance of $9,909.92 at the end of three years. You'll find that the interest rate of the transaction jumps to 15.39 per cent—as compared to the 13.5 per cent quoted rate and the 14.34 per cent true rate for 30 full years. The effect is even worse if the mortgage is paid off in less than three years, but mellows out rapidly if the mortgage is held for longer periods.

It all means that to really compare mortgage offers you have to consider not only the interest rate and the up-front fees but also the consequences of paying off the mortgage if you don't intend to see it through its full term. And don't fool yourself—extremely few *final* monthly payments are ever made.

ASSUMPTIONS

If your mortgage is assumable, you may yet escape those early pay-off penalties. If a buyer can take over your home's mortgage as well as the home itself, your mortgage is assumable. Your successor would take responsibility for making all further monthly payments on the mortgage.

Assumption is another advantage government-guaranteed mortgages give to borrowers. Most of these mortgages can be assumed at the *original interest rate.* Many non-government-guaranteed mortgages are also assumable but often at a higher interest rate.

Homes with assumable mortgages are much easier to sell. The buyer will avoid origination fees (although nongovenments may have equivalent "assumption fees") and, if the general level of interest rates has risen, may get some very cheap money. Sellers of homes with assumable mortgages, on the other hand, should be aware of the value of their mortgages and should add a portion of the mortgage's value onto the price of their homes.

For example, imagine you obtained a new $55,000, 30-year, 8.5 per cent assumable mortgage six years ago. The monthly payment on this mortgage would be $422.90; the current balance would be $51,884.34 (find the present value of a 24-year, 8.5 per cent mortgage with a monthly payment of $422.90). This is the amount a buyer could apply to the price of your home by assuming your mortgage.

If the buyer's only alternative is to take a 14 per cent mortgage to buy another home down the street, borrowing $51,884.34 would cost about $200 a month more—$627.54. Obviously your mortgage has some value attached to it.

THE HIDDEN VALUE OF LOW-INTEREST MORTGAGES

To determine the value added to your mortgage by the change in interest rates, use our Present Value of a Series of Remittances formulas to determine the true present value of your mortgage at today's interest rates. In the previous example, a mortgage with 24 remaining years of $422.90 payments would have a present value of $34,964.75 at 14 per cent interest. This is *nearly $17,000* less than the balance a purchaser could apply to the price of your home. Consequently, you should attempt to increase the price of your home by at least half that much—otherwise you are giving away that value.

Alternatively, with some mortgages you can go to the lender and offer to pay off the loan at a discount. Lenders are well aware of the present value of your stream of remittances at current interest rates and they are often quite willing to *take less than the full balance* to close out low-interest rate mortgages. Unfortunately, this tactic doesn't work with most government-guaranteed mortgages, for reasons that are way too complicated to get into here.

One of the biggest mistakes a home owner can make is to sell his or her home and pay off a low-interest loan at full value without first negotiating with the lender—particularly if a prepayment penalty is involved. Do your negotiating before you sell the home. That way you can tell the lender that if a lower prepayment balance cannot be negotiated, you won't sell. Lenders *badly* need to get the money tied up in your low-interest loan back out at higher rates. Therefore, if you can convince them you understand the value of your mortgage, they will negotiate. The amounts of money you are dealing with here are usually in the thousands of dollars, so it's well worth hiring a lawyer or accountant to help you negotiate if you don't feel you can do it yourself.

On the other hand, if you are a home buyer rather than a seller, beat the real estate bushes for a home with an assumable mortgage. Most people who have this kind of mortgage have no idea how much it is worth. *There is no cheaper way to borrow large amounts of money than to assume someone's low-interest mortgage at face value.*

ADJUSTABLE-RATE MORTGAGES

Another significant advantage of assuming an old mortgage is that it will probably have a fixed interest rate. Recently lenders have become reluctant to offer standard fixed-rate mortgages and instead are pushing *adjustable-rate mortgages* on borrowers. With this kind of mortgage, the interest rate you pay rises or falls with the general level of interest rates according to a predetermined formula—recalculation typically occurs every one to three years. At each recalculation the borrower's monthly payment changes, sometimes drastically. The calculation uses the new interest rate, the number of years remaining to pay off the mortgage, and the outstanding balance.

The standard fixed-rate mortgage has fallen out of lenders' favor because of the big increase in interest rates during late 1970s and early 1980s. Lenders have millions of dollars of mortgages outstanding at interest rates *below* what it now costs them to borrow money. They are losing their jobs over these mortgages. Rather than continue to risk rising rates, lenders want borrowers to share the risk by allowing the interest rate on their mortgages to be adjusted periodically.

The standard fixed-rate mortgage definitely has features that favor borrowers over lenders. The borrower can pay off the loan at any time. In some cases this may involve a prepayment penalty, as we have seen, but often it doesn't. The lender, on the other hand, can't demand prepayment except under special conditions agreed upon when the mortgage is signed (such as, perhaps, if the home is sold.)

If interest rates go up, the lender has reason to want to get out of the mortgage but can't. If rates go down, on the other hand, the borrower always has the option of *refinancing* the loan by borrowing, at the new lower rates, enough to pay off the loan. Thus, with a standard fixed-rate mortgage, borrowers are able to take advantage of significantly lower rates, but lenders usually can't take advantage of higher rates.

This is the problem the adjustable-rate mortgage is supposed to solve.

CALCULATING ADJUSTABLE RATES

The formula that lenders use for determining the interest rate on adjustable-rate mortgages is based on an *index* interest rate. For example, many lenders peg their adjustable-rate mortgages to the rate quoted for 26-week Treasury bills, which changes weekly. The lender will add a *premium* to the rate of the chosen index. The sum determines the rate the borrower will pay. For example, if a lender's index rate and premium were 10.6 per cent and 4 per cent respectively, the lender's adjustable-rate mortgages would carry a 14.6 per cent rate.

The index and premium actually used vary from lender to lender.

Index and Premium Differences

When comparing adjustable-rate mortgages, ask each lender for a table that shows the level, for the last five to ten years, of the index the lender is using. The different indices lenders use vary by as much as several percentage points. Theoretically, lenders using indices with relatively high rates will charge relatively low premiums, while lenders using indices with relatively low rates will charge high premiums.

To determine which lender is offering the best rate, compare what interest rates would have been paid had the mortgage agreement been signed five or ten years earlier. The future relationships of the various indices, of course, could change; but usually they'll follow historical patterns.

In addition to noting the level of the index, find out whether the lender's index is averaged over time. Some lenders, for example, use the last weekly T-bill quote as an index. An index based on average rates over a one-year period will be much less volatile than a index based on weekly rates. If you take a mortgage that's based on weekly rates, the interest you pay will depend entirely on what the index reads during the week your mortgage comes up for recalculation. This could be either much higher or much lower than the average rate for the year. If you are a gambler, you might enjoy having a mortgage based on this kind of an index. Most people will prefer an index based on average rates, however.

TEASER RATES

The major problem with adjustable-rate mortgages is that they give unscrupulous lenders a whole new quiverful of tricks to use on unsuspecting borrowers. The worst of these is the *teaser rate*.

Lenders who quote adjustable-rate mortgages at a rate lower than what their formula specifies are using teaser rates. These mortgages look like good deals to unsuspecting borrowers because they seem to carry very low rates in comparison to those for fixed-rate mortgages. However, these low rates apply *only during the first calculation period* of the mortgage. In later periods the true rate specified by formula will be used. And, as you might expect, these true rates aren't much different from those quoted for fixed-rate mortgages.

Lenders who offer teaser rates use origination fees, in a slightly different manner from the method we looked at earlier, to lower the quoted interest rate during the first calculation period of the mortgage. Instead of using such a fee to reduce the quoted interest rate of the entire 30-year mortgage, they concentrate the effect of the fee in the mortgage's first calculation period. Consequently the quoted teaser rate is very deceptive indeed.

Say you borrowed $50,000 on a 30-year mortgage with annual adjustments and that the lender's index and premium indicate the rate should be 14.7 per cent. Rather than quoting that rate to you, however, the lender might quote a rate of 12.5 per cent with a 2-1/8 per cent origination fee; or even 10 per cent with a 4-3/8 per cent origination fee. Both these combinations allow the lender to earn more than 14.7 per cent during the first year of the mortgage.

The Math behind the Teaser

To find the true first-year rate of an adjustable-rate mortgage, use the Present Value formulas with the quoted interest rate and amount borrowed to find the monthly payment of the mortgage. Then use that monthly payment figure and change the number of years to discover the present value of the mortgage at the end of the first calculation period.

Now switch to a goliah template. Enter the beginning balance of the mortgage. Treat the origination fee as a remittance made at the beginning of the first month of the loan and treat the monthly payment as a remittance made at the end of each month. Adjust the interest rate and recalculate until you find an interest rate that gives you the correct present value at the end of the first calculation period.

For example, with a $50,000, 30-year, 12.5 per cent, annually adjusted mortgage, you would enter 50,000 as the present value, 12.5 as the interest rate, and 30 as the number of years. This would give you a monthly payment of $533.63. Next enter that amount in the formula, change the number of years to 29, and ask for the present value. This will give you $49,837.46.

Now get out a clean goliah worksheet. Set it up for one year of monthly remittances. Enter 50,000 as the beginning balance, $ − 50,000 * .02125 as a remittance at the beginning of the first period (this is the 2-1/8 per cent origination fee), and the monthly payment of $ − 533.63 as the remittance at the end of the period. Since the origination fee is only made once, put a 0 in the cell immediately beneath it.

Copy or replicate the formulas through the twelfth period and bring the beginning balance formula down one additional row. Now vary the interest rate until that final beginning balance, which represents the balance of the mortgage at the end of one year, is close to $49,837. You'll find 14.8 per cent is as close as you can get with three digits. This is the true interest rate for the first year of the mortgage.

DON'T BET YOUR HOUSE ON IT

Serious problems occur for borrowers when the lender determines whether or not they *qualify* for a mortgage based on a teaser rate. To qualify, you must demonstrate that your mortgage payments, property taxes, and homeowners' insurance will be less than a certain portion of your income, usually 25 per cent. If your total housing costs take up more of your monthly income than that, a legitimate lender won't give you the loan, because it would be a hardship for you to pay it off.

At the teaser rate we just looked at, your monthly payment is only $533.63. If taxes and insurance were $150, you would need a monthly income of $2,735, using a 25 per cent qualification level, to get the loan. But at the *real* rate of the mortgage the monthly payment should be $624.23; your monthly income to qualify should be $3,097—13 per cent higher than at the teaser rate!

What are the consequences? Home buyers borrow more money than they should. When their mortgage payments rise after the teaser period is over—as they almost inevitably will, even if the general level of interest rates falls slightly, it becomes a hardship to gather the funds to make the monthly payment. The hardship must be endured; or the house sold, usually at a loss after considering a real estate agent's fees. Or you can default on the mortgage and lose your down payment or more. A lender who lets you have a loan you don't really qualify for *isn't doing you a favor*. Such lenders are just trying to stay in business—in the face of unbearable interest rates—any way they can.

Tips About Caps

Most adjustable rate mortgages have *caps* or limits on the number of percentage points the interest rate can change from calculation period to calculation period. Some have a cap on the maximum interest rate the mortgage can ever carry. Some have floors under which the rate can never fall.

Compare the *maximum possible rate* an adjustable mortgage offers with what's available in fixed-rate mortgages. It will make you feel better about taking the fixed-rate mortgage. If your lender indicates it is unlikely interest rates will ever go that high, laugh. If the lender really believed that, he or she would be better off getting you to sign a fixed-rate mortgage.

In general, caps are a good thing for borrowers, as long as they apply to the *interest rate*. Some lenders put the cap on the monthly payment rather than on the interest rate. In this situation the actual interest rate can rise to any level. It can even rise high enough that your capped monthly payment is not paying even the interest on your loan, much less the principal. In this situation the mortgage undergoes *negative amortization*, which means the additional unpaid interest is *added to* the outstanding balance of your mortgage. After a year of payments under these conditions, you owe *more than* you did at the beginning of the year.

Graduated payment mortgages also have this feature. In this kind of mortgage, the monthly payment rises each year according to a set schedule. In the early years of the mortgage, the payments aren't high enough to cover accrued interest; thus, during the early years of the mortgage, the outstanding balance *grows*. Later on your payments get high enough to pay off both the interest and the principal. This kind of mortgage may be perfect for someone whose income will increase over the years, but it carries a lot of risk if things don't go according to plan. If you want to look at the math of this kind of mortgage, get out a goliah worksheet and use the mortgage's formula to change the monthly payment every year.

Up in ARMs

The adjustable-rate mortgage is a recent development. It's still a bit too soon to comment on its long-term viability.

Nonetheless, it's clear that the adjustable-rate mortgage was born after investors and mortgage lenders became unwilling to take all the risk associated with the volatile interest rates of recent years.

It is unfortunate that, for the most part, borrowers have been *tricked* into accepting this risk by means of teaser rates. It is certain that many fewer adjustable mortgages would have been written had lenders been more forthright about the true interest rates being charged. Some of this business would have gone to fixed-rate mortgages, the rest would simply have disappeared. The home-construction industry would have felt the impact.

As more and more homeowners find that their monthly payment—and quality of life—hinges on interest-rate indices, political pressure to keep interest rates as low as possible will become widespread. The big questions are how long it will take for this to happen, and how many homeowners will suffer unbearably high rates in the meantime.

However, given the home mortgage industry's record for shooting itself in the foot in recent years, it would not be a great surprise, I suppose, if interest rates fell precipitously just as a majority of homes were converted to adjustable-rate mortgages. That way, what the industry lost when rates were rising it would be unable to regain as rates fell.

But no one knows for sure. No one can predict the future with certainty. That's what puts all the fun in life.

ESCROW ACCOUNTS

Anyone who has ever had a home mortgage is familiar with the term *escrow account*. Those of you who are new to this stuff need to become familiar with it, however.

Most lenders insist on protecting their mortgage investment in your home from the taxman and from acts of God. To ensure that you are paying property taxes on time and that your homeowner's insurance is paid up, your lender will collect additional funds from you each month over and above your principal and interest payments. The lender will hold onto these funds until your tax and insurance bills are due. Then the lender will pay these bills for you.

Escrow accounts cause several minor problems. First of all, if you enter someone's monthly payment into one of our time-value formulas and forget to subtract the escrow amount, all the answers will be wrong. The time value formulas in this book, like all such formulas, are for a loan's principal and interest only—escrow amounts are never included in the "remittance."

Secondly, because the amount you pay for taxes and insurance changes from year to year, the monthly payment you make to the lender will also usually change from year to year. Some people think this means they have an adjustable-rate mortgage. All that's being adjusted, however, is the escrow amount. You only have an adjustable-rate mortgage if the *interest rate* changes.

The biggest problem with escrow accounts is that precious few lenders *pay interest* on the money they are holding in escrow for you. You can be sure they are earning interest on the money, however.

Unless you are the type who might go out and spend the money you'll need for property taxes and homeowners insurance on Cabbage Patch dolls, you should ask your lender to drop the escrow requirement on your mortgage. If you have a history of paying your bills on time and if your equity in your home is 20 per cent or more, most lenders will agree to do so.

Questions to Ask about Loans and Mortgages

Here's a summary of the questions you should ask when shopping for a large commercial loan or a real estate mortgage. Time invested in shopping for money is much better spent than time devoted to shopping for the best deal on Wheaties, Sonys, or Lawn-Boys.

Questions related to all loans and mortgages:

- what interest rate/term combinations are available?
- is there an origination fee?
- are there any other fees?
- is there a prepayment penalty?
- is the mortgage assumable (home mortgages)?
- is an escrow account required (home mortgages)?
- can I afford the monthly payments (home mortgages)?
- is an offseting balance required (commercial loans)?
- can I earn a return higher than the interest rate (commercial loans)?

Additional questions for adjustable rate mortgages:

- how often is the payment recalculated?
- what is the interest rate indexed on?
- is the index an average over time?
- how much of a premium is added to the index rate?
- what would the interest rate be now using this formula?
- what is the true first-year interest rate?
- are there any caps?
- is negative amortization possible?
- can I afford the *maximum possible* monthly payment?

LOANS AND MORTGAGES: STUDY QUESTIONS

1. How is interest calculated under the *discount method*? under the *add-on method*? What is deceptive about these techniques?

2. How do *origination fees*, *buy-downs*, and *points* affect the true interest rate of a loan or mortgage? What's an *offsetting balance* and how does it affect the true interest rate?

3. Are *prepayment penalties* an advantage for the lender or for the borrower? When buying a house, why should you search out homes with *assumable* mortgages?

4. Why have lenders become so interested in *adjustable-rate mortgages*? What's a *teaser rate* and what's so deceptive about it? What's a *cap*? What's *negative amortization*?

INVESTMENTS

INVESTMENTS: BACKGROUND AND TUTORIAL

"Why do you rob banks?" someone once asked a notorious criminal. "Because that's where the money is," the criminal responded.

What we often forget, though it probably would make no difference to criminals, is that the money in banks and other financial institutions belongs not to the institution but to investors. The "lenders" whose tricks we studied in Chapter 6 get the funds they lend by *borrowing them* from pension funds, from widows and orphans who have received big life-insurance payments, from big bingo winners, and, perhaps to a lesser extent, from the rest of us.

The well-being of financial institutions depends on their being able to borrow more cheaply than they lend. If they sometimes use tricks to make interest rates look small to loan customers, you can bet they will sometimes use tricks to make interest rates look big to investment customers. As mentioned in Chapter 6, there are no "Truth-in-Investing" laws to complement "Truth-in-Lending." Thus, if anything, depositors have to be even more careful.

There are three basic kinds of investments you can put your wealth into—non-interest-bearing, interest-bearing, and income-producing. Let's look at non-interest-bearing investments first.

Non-Interest-Bearing Investments

Investments that don't earn interest are really outside the scope of this book, but I think it's important that we acknowledge that they exist.

125

For an individual, this kind of investment would include a home, car, clothing, furniture—anything that had a useful economic life but was not used to produce income.

Since the beginnings of the human race, our philosophers have peeked and poked and thought and studied, looking for the meaning of life. What's it all about? There are thousands of answers. But damn few philosophers have decided we are here primarily to collect interest.

The mathematics of interest are interesting. They are useful. But don't let them consume you. There is nothing more intrinsically boring than sitting around watching interest collect.

Art, on the other hand, doesn't pay interest, but it will enrich you. It takes a whole day and quite a few dollars to see *Nicholas Nickleby*, but you'll savor it forever. There are many things you can invest in that can't possibly have any financial return, but that in itself is not a good reason to avoid them.

Then there are things people invest in hoping the price will go up and they can sell out at a profit. Such things include gold, gems, and beer can collections. For a person to profit from such investments, the price of the item must increase enough to offset the interest that could have been earned had the money been put elsewhere. Sometimes this actually happens.

The gut appeal of these investments is that they are supposed to keep up with inflation. As we have seen, the real interest rate earned by an investment depends more on inflation than on the general level of interest. The problem is that when inflation is rampant everyone wants into these kinds of investments and the price of the item rises. When inflation disappears everyone wants out and the price falls.

In early 1980, after a long upward climb, the price of gold was approaching $1,000 an ounce. Investors everywhere were kicking themselves that they hadn't put all their wealth in gold when it was available for $35 an ounce. The most cogent comment about trying to profit from the situation, however, came from the fellow who admitted, "All I know is that if I'd ever had any gold I would have sold it a long time ago."

ONE YEAR OR THREE?

Another interest-related question that often arises in day-to-day spending has to do with whether it's better to pay things such as insurance premiums monthly, quarterly, or annually. Is it better to buy a one-year subscription to a magazine or a three-year subscription?

One of the scientific journals my wife subscribes to offers a one-year renewal for $43.50, a two-year renewal for $78.50, and a three-year renewal for $117.50. Which one is the best deal?

To solve this problem, set up a goliah worksheet with three one-year periods. Enter −43.50, the one-year price, as a remittance at the start of each period. That is what we'll have to pay if we don't invest any other money with the magazine. Now enter 78.50, the two-year price, as a beginning balance and change the interest rate until the third year beginning balance is 0. This is the interest rate we can earn on the amount over 43.50 by letting the journal use it for one year. You'll find that the rate is more than 24 per cent.

Now enter the three-year price, 117.50, as the beginning balance and change the interest rate until the balance at the beginning of the *fourth* year is 0. This is the rate our excess payment could earn with the journal's three-year offer. You'll find this rate is only about 11.5 per cent. The two-year subscription is the best deal, assuming the journal's subscription price doesn't change during the period.

One final non-interest-bearing investment we should mention is traveler's checks. Not only do you not earn interest on these; often you must pay a fee for the privilege of letting the issuer use your money. Don't save traveler's checks for your next trip unless you enjoy watching American Express's profits grow. And don't be like the dumbos in the advertisements who travel with all their worldly possessions in one pocket. Put a little in one pocket, a little in another pocket, a little in your suitcase, and a little in your shoe or other private place—and don't forget where you put any of it.

Interest-Bearing Investments

This book is *not a guide* to investments. There are plenty of other books that describe all the various types of things you can invest in. Those books can help you decide which investment, if any, is right for you. Our goal here is to become aware of the kinds of things that must be considered when determining the true interest rate offered by an investment.

There are two basic kinds of interest-bearing investments, accounts and paper. An account is generally used for investments that you want to make deposits to and withdrawals from. Checking accounts, credit union accounts, money market funds, and so on, are all examples. Interest-bearing paper, on the other hand, is for investments you want to leave pretty much undisturbed. Examples are certificates of deposit, U.S. treasury securities such as T-bills, and corporate bonds.

The calculation of interest seems pretty straightforward. You take the principal, multiply it by the annual interest rate, and then multiply that figure by the amount of time the money has been earning interest. Assuming that you deposit the same amount of principal at two different institutions paying the same interest rate and leave it there the same amount of time, you should be able to withdraw the same amount of money, right? It all makes sense, but it's not nearly that easy.

ACCOUNTS

There are three major reasons why the interest paid by two different accounts might vary. They are *compounding* differences, *crediting* differences, and *calculation* differences.

COMPOUNDING

We discussed compounding at length way back in Chapter 2. The more frequently interest is compounded, the higher the effective interest rate. As you know, the reason frequent compounding earns you more is because it allows you to earn interest on interest. An account that pays interest quarterly won't have anything in it but the principal after two months, but an account with monthly compounding will have both the principal and the first two months' interest.

CREDITING

Few institutions that say they offer "daily compounding" actually put interest into your account every day. The money is placed in your account monthly or even less often. Some gnome inside a computer somewhere is supposed to calculate your interest *as if* it had been placed in your account every day, but it doesn't really happen that way.

Financial institutions call the process by which interest is actually placed in your account *crediting*. The amount of time it takes from one crediting to the next is the *crediting period*. Crediting frequency isn't as important as compounding frequency, but it does make a big difference when you go to close an account.

At most institutions an account must still be open on the day of crediting or it won't earn *any* interest for the current crediting period. For example, say you have an account that is compounded daily, but interest is paid quarterly. If July 1 is the next crediting date and on June 20 you close the account, you'll lose all interest earned between April 1 and June 20.

You can leave a minimum balance in the account until interest is credited, or you can just wait. Be careful of this gotcha when closing accounts because you're moving, because you want to switch financial institutions, or even because you want to move your money to a different type of account. Always close accounts right after interest has been credited. You can figure out how often and when interest is credited to your accounts by looking at the statements your financial institution sends you.

PRINCIPAL CALCULATIONS

There are three major methods financial institutions use to determine the amount of *principal* on which interest will be paid.

All three methods of calculating your principal come up with the same result if there is a balance in your account the first day of a crediting period and you leave it undisturbed until the first day of the next period. Very significant differences arise, however, when you make withdrawals or deposits. Here are the three different methods and how they work.

Day of deposit to day of withdrawl: With this method, interest is calculated using the true end-of-day balance of the account. If compounding is less frequent than daily, the average end-of-day balance during the compounding period is used. This is the most frequently used method of calculating interest and the most favorable method for depositors.

Beginning of month to end of crediting period: In this case, interest is calculated only on funds that are in an account at the beginning of a month and left in the account until the end of the crediting period. This method is a favorite of credit unions. It significantly lowers the high interest rate they usually quote. If you had $3,000 in an account at the beginning of a six-month crediting period, added $1,000 two weeks later, and withdrew $500 on the next-to-last day of the period, you would earn six months interest on the original $3,000, five months interest on $500 of the $1,000 deposited later, and no interest at all on the $500 withdrawn before the end of the period—even though it was on deposit well over five months. If you have money in an account that calculates interest this way, it's best to make deposits near the end of the month and make withdrawals only right after a crediting period ends.

Low balance method: This method calculates interest on the lowest balance in the account during the period. In the above example, interest would be paid on $3,000. This is the worst method for depositors. Avoid it.

In addition to these three methods, some institutions use methods known as FIFO and LIFO. If you find an institution using one of these methods and you have a couple of hours to burn, ask an officer of the institution to explain to you how the method works. (If enough of you do this, the few remaining institutions using these methods will switch to something else.)

TIME CALCULATIONS

In addition to the three major ways of calculating the principal, there are two major ways of calculating time. The *ordinary* method assumes there are 360 days in a year. The *exact* method assumes there are 365 (366 in leap years).

The ordinary method favors depositors. For example, if an account pays 8 per cent interest with daily compounding, the interest rate per period (one day) would be .0222 per cent (8/360) with ordinary interest, but only .0219 per cent (8/365) with exact interest. With ordinary interest and daily compounding, the true interest rate you'll get will actually be higher than the quoted rate, since you'll get 365 days of the 360-day rate.

If you want to compare accounts at different institutions, the easiest way to proceed as far as the time calculation goes is to ask what the interest rate is *per compounding period*. Multiply that times the number of compounding periods and you'll know the true rate. Or better yet, use the following formula to find the *effective annual yield*, which takes into account both the method of calculating time and the number of compounding periods:

Where:

Y = effective annual yield as a decimal fraction
Q = number of compounding periods per year
I1 = interest rate per period as a decimal fraction

Y = ((1+I1)^Q)-1

Another way many institutions lower the true interest rate they are paying is by putting a *hold* on deposits. This happens when you deposit a check drawn on another bank. Some withhold interest for just one or two business days—the time usually required for the institution to receive payment for the check from the Federal Reserve or other clearing bank. Others withhold interest for longer times, some for much longer.

In addition to loss of interest, a major problem with a hold is that the deposit cannot be withdrawn until the holding period is over. This can be painful for the depositor, especially since the bank already has the money.

The good news is that in some regions of the country, such as here in Kansas City, institutions almost never put a hold on deposits.

HERE'S YOUR FREE GIFT

Some financial institutions offer gifts to people opening new accounts. The thing to beware of is that sometimes the gifts are *in lieu of interest*. That means that instead of getting interest you get the "gift."

Now here's a little gift for those of you who have made it all the way through this much of Chapter 7—a list of things to ask when comparing interest-bearing accounts:

Questions related to interest-bearing accounts:

- how often is interest compounded?
- what is the rate *per compounding period*?
- how often is interest credited to the account?
- how is the principal calculated?
- what is the "hold" policy on deposits?
- is the account insured?

INTEREST-BEARING PAPER

The major kinds of interest-bearing paper available to individual investors are certificates of deposit, which are issued by banks and other financial institutions; Treasury bills, which are issued by the U.S. government; and bonds and notes, which are issued by all levels of government as well as by many corporations. Paper tends to pay a higher rate of interest than accounts.

CERTIFICATES OF DEPOSIT

Certificates of deposit are issued by financial institutions. They mature after a specific period of time, such as one year, 30 months, or four years.

One big advantage certificates of deposit have over other types of interest-bearing paper is that their earnings can be compounded at the certificate's interest rate. (If you prefer you can also have the interest paid directly to you.) Most other interest-bearing paper pays interest as it comes due, making compounding at the paper's higher rates impossible.

A disadvantage of certificates of deposit is that, at least in the sizes available to most individuals, they aren't negotiable. This means that if you need to liquidate a certificate of deposit before it matures, you have to pay an interest penalty. Typically the penalty is six months worth of interest—even if you withdraw the funds before six months have passed.

TREASURY BILLS

To finance the national debt, the U.S. Treasury issues several types of securities. These are called *bills*, *notes*, and *bonds*. The primary difference among the three is their maturity. Bills are issued in 13-week (91 days; 3 months), 26-week (182 days; 6 months), and 52-week (364 days; 1 year) maturities. Notes can have a maturity of one to ten years; bonds ten years or more.

Government securities offer investors three main advantages. First, they are considered to be free of risk. Second, interest earned on them is exempt from state (but not federal) income taxes. Third, they are traded in large volumes in the open market and consequently can be "cashed in" at any time without penalty (other than a brokerage commission).

The Treasury also issues *savings bonds*, which are available to individuals in small denominations. Savings bonds have additional advantages—interest is tax-deferred and, like the interest earned on a certificate of deposit, is compounded. They can be purchased and redeemed at any bank without fees or commissions. Nowadays, savings bonds pay an interest rate that is adjusted every six months to 85 per cent of the average yield on five-year Treasury notes—a rate usually competitive with money market funds. However, savings bonds have to be held for at least six months before they can be cashed at all and they must be held more than five years to be cashed without significant interest penalties. Interest is credited semiannually; make sure you redeem savings bonds soon after a six-month anniversary.

Treasury notes and bonds are priced and trade just like corporate bonds. We'll discuss them further later in this chapter. Treasury bills, on the other hand, are an unusual breed of paper.

Discount Interest

First of all, T-bills use the "ordinary" method of calculating time—a year is assumed to have 360 days. Next, T-bills don't pay interest directly. Investors earn a return because bills are issued at a discount from their face value. At maturity they can be redeemed at full face value. Consequently, T-bills are quoted with *discount interest rates*. As mentioned in Chapter 6, a discount rate is always lower than the true interest rate.

For example, you buy a one-year T-bill with a face value of $10,000 for $9,000.00. (For purposes of this example we'll assume you walked into a Federal Reserve Bank and bought the bill without a commission fee; if you buy through a bank or broker you'll have to pay a commission that will raise the price and lower the true interest rate.) The interest rate quoted for the bill would be about 10 per cent—you bought the bill for 10 per cent less than its face value.

However, we all know by now that true interest rates are calculated on the present value of the transaction, not on the future value. Since your $9,000 investment will earn $1,000, the true interest rate, or *yield*, is 1000/9000 or 11.1 per cent.

The Time Zone

Why is the Treasury's rate quote *about* 10 per cent and not *exactly* 10 per cent? Because the Treasury calculates the discount as if a year has only 360 days, while the bill is outstanding for exactly 364 days. This makes the quoted rate even lower—9.89 per cent. A T-bill's true yield is always higher than the quoted interest rate it carries. This is because of the discount method of calculation and because of the funny time calculations.

This works to the advantage of T-bill investors. You actually earn 11.1 per cent on an investment that appears to offer 9.89 per cent. On the other hand, it works to the disadvantage of taxpayers. They think their government is borrowing money at 9.89 per cent instead of 11.1 per cent.

(Note: If you have an adjustable-rate mortgage based on T-bills, is the rate based on the quoted T-bill rate or the true T-bill rate? Presumably your lender is smart enough to get a bigger premium if the index is the quoted rate. The thing to beware of is being shown quoted T-bill rates as an example of the level of the index and then finding your mortgage is based on the true T-bill rate.)

To find the true interest rate offered by a T-bill or other discount security, use the following formulas:

Where:

```
F = face value of paper
P = price of paper

I = true annual interest rate as a decimal fraction
D = discount interest rate as a decimal fraction
YDAY = length of year in days (T-bills = 360)
IDAY = length of investment in days

F = P / (1 - (D*(IDAY/YDAY)))
P = F * (1 - (D*(IDAY/YDAY)))
D = (1-(P/F)) * (YDAY/IDAY)

I = (365 * D) / (YDAY - (D*IDAY))
D = (YDAY * I) / (365 + (I*IDAY))
```

BONDS AND NOTES

Bonds and notes are available from a variety of sources, including the U.S. Treasury, major corporations, some special agencies of the federal government, and state and local governments.

These securities typically have a face value of $1,000 and pay a predetermined rate of interest semiannually. The rate of interest paid is often referred to as the *coupon*. Once upon a time, bonds were issued with a set of coupons that allowed the bond holder to collect interest. The coupons had to be clipped off the bond when interest was due and presented to the issuer. In the jargon of the money market, such securities and their successors are called *coupons*.

Unlike discount securities, coupons are issued at a price equal to, or at least very close to, their face (or *par*) value (almost always $1,000). The coupon interest rate associated with a particular issue is set according to the prevailing interest rate at the time of issue.

If you look at listing of U.S. Treasury bond prices in a newspaper, what you'll see will look something like this:

rate	maturity	high	low	last	chg	yield
11-3/4s	Feb 2001	94.15	93.7	94.15	+.25	12.55
13-1/8s	May 2001	104.2	102.22	104.2	+.27	12.54
15-3/4s	Nov 2001	122.8	120.27	122.8	+1.2	12.56

The listing shows prices for three different issues of Treasury bonds. These bonds were all issued in 1981 with 20-year maturities. As you can tell by looking at the rate and maturity columns, interest rates were rising during 1981. The Treasury was able to sell these bonds with an interest rate of 11-3/4 per cent in February, but in May a 13-1/8 per cent rate was required, and by November the Treasury had to offer 15-3/4 per cent.

Deciphering Bond Prices

The next three columns are high, low, and last asking prices for these bonds. The prices are a little tricky for a couple of reasons. First, the number after the decimal point represents 32nds. For example, the high price of the first bond was 94-15/32nds. Secondly, the prices shown have to be multiplied by 10 to arrive at the true price of a single bond. Thus, the high price of the February bond, in dollars and cents, was $944.69.

The little *s* after the interest rate indicates interest is paid semiannually. Interest payments are calculated on the face value of the bond, not on the price. If you bought that February bond, for example, you could expect to collect $117.50 in interest (11.75 per cent of $1,000) from the government each year ($58.75 every six months, actually) until 2001, at which time you would get your $1,000 back.

Since you didn't pay $1,000 for the bond, however, but only $944.69, the true interest rate you would earn would be higher than the 11.75 per cent coupon. First of all, the semiannual interest payments represent about 12.44 per cent interest on your $944.69. Secondly, the difference between the $944.69 you paid for the bond and the $1,000 you will get back at redemption can be considered a lump-sum time-value transaction. If, for example, it would take 17 years before the bond could be redeemed, our Time Value of a Lump Sum formulas will tell you the interest rate involved here is 0.33 per cent. The gain is considered a *capital gain* for income tax purposes. Capital gains are taxed at a lower rate than other income.

Finding the True Yield of a Bond

The last column in the price table is labeled "yield." This is the interest rate the bond pays if you combine the simple-interest coupon payments with the compound-interest lump-sum value. The yield is calculated by considering the interest payments and final redemption to be a stream of remittances. Using a spreadsheet's @NPV function, you could find the yield of a bond by adjusting the interest rate until the present value of the stream of remittances was equal to the price of the bond. Using a goliah worksheet, you could find the yield by including the price of the bond as a negative remittance and adjusting the interest rate until the future value was $1,000.

A significant problem with these methods is that they are only truly accurate on two days of the year—the days interest is paid. Otherwise the fact that you won't have to wait a full six months for the first interest payment throws the calculation off a little. And because of the well-known (by now, we hope) remittance-at-end-of-period assumption of time-value formulas, the @NPV method also figures that somebody else, not you, gets the interest paid on the day you purchase the bond.

The only easy way to figure out the actual yield of a bond is to look in the newspaper.

Going back to our list of bond prices, notice that the yields of all three bonds are about equal, even though the coupon rates are very different. Price differences make up for this. The November bond would cost $1,222.50. You would receive big semiannual interest payments of $78.75 with this bond. However, when you redeemed the bond you would get only $1,000. You would have a capital loss of $222.50, which works out to a compound interest rate of −1.18 percent.

Holding to Maturity

Thus, when you buy a bond on the open market intending to hold it till maturity, you have to consider two things. How much simple interest will the bond earn, based on the price you have to pay and the bond's coupon rate, and how much compound interest will you gain, or lose, based on the bond's price and its face value.

Bonds with coupons very near the going interest rate will be priced very close to 100 and will have almost all of their yield available through the coupon. Bonds with coupons much lower or higher than the going interest rate, on the other hand, will have more yield tied up in capital gains or losses. Since this portion can earn at a locked-in compound rate, some investors seek out bonds with low coupons. Some bonds, in fact, pay no interest whatsoever. They are called zero-coupon bonds. All "interest" is paid when the bond is redeemed. (However, the IRS likes to tax it as it accrues.)

As long as you intend to hold a bond to maturity and you are satisfied with the interest rate you can obtain with a bond, the only thing that can go wrong is the issuer *defaulting*. This means you get no further interest payments and no redemption. When a company appears near default, the price of its bonds will fall drastically.

The Consequences of Selling Out

If you intend to resell a bond in the open market before maturity, however, the *yield of your bond transaction as a whole* will be dependent on what happens to interest rates while you are holding the bond. It is impossible to lock-in the yield printed in the newspaper unless you are willing to hold the bond to maturity.

If interest rates rise while you are holding the bond, the bond's price will fall. When you sell it you will have a capital loss. This will lower your true yield.

And if, on the other hand, interest rates fall, your bond's price will rise. You will have a bigger capital gain. The true yield of the transaction will be more than you had expected.

If bonds intrigue you as an investment opportunity, don't let this little introduction be your sole guide. As you can see, investing in bonds is quite complex and has many hidden ramifications. Learn all you can before you pay your first commission.

Income-Producing Investments

Like non-interest-bearing investments, income-producing investments are really beyond the scope of this book, but let's take a quick look at them anyhow.

When you invest in something like stocks or real estate, you should expect a higher return than you can get investing elsewhere. You are taking more risk and you're doing more work. Even IBM is more likely to go bankrupt than the U.S. government is.

The advantage of stock and real estate investments is that their intrinsic value has at least some potential of keeping up with inflation. Dividends aren't the only source of income. The dividend paid by a stock, as a percentage of the stock's price, is almost always less than the going interest rate. This is because companies are expected to grow. Dividends and the value of the stock are expected to be higher in the future.

There are many other income-producing investments. The thing you always need to consider is whether the investment will earn enough extra, compared to what you could get by collecting interest, to be worth your time and trouble.

Backward Is Easy

The sad part, friends, is that you'll never really know what interest rate you've earned on a transaction until the future value is at hand. When the transaction is history, you can finally look back and know with certainty the effect of taxes and the effect of inflation. You'll know whether whomever you lent your money to really did pay off; you'll know exactly what alternative investments would have paid. You'll know what the right decision *would have* been.

But the real purpose of the formulas and mathematical techniques presented in this book is to help you peer into the future. They're like little flashlights helping you grope through darkness. May they always warn you of the deep dark pits.

INVESTMENTS: STUDY QUESTIONS

1. What are the three major reasons that the actual interest paid by two accounts that have the same interest rate might differ?

2. What do you have to be careful about when closing an interest-bearing account?

3. What's the difference between "ordinary" and "exact" time?

4. Is the interest rate quoted for Treasury bills higher or lower than their true interest rate? Why?

5. How much would it cost to buy a U.S. Treasury note priced at 89.23? If you bought this note and interest rates began to drop, would the price go up or down? If you resold the note at the lower interest rate level, would your true yield on the transaction be more or less than the yield quoted when you bought the bond?

APPENDIX A

INTEREST-RATE FORMULA SUMMARY

Where:

    PV = present value
    FV = future value
   PMT = remittance amount of an annuity

   TAX = your income tax rate as a decimal fraction
   INF = annual inflation rate as a decimal fraction

     I = true annual interest rate as a decimal fraction
     D = discount interest rate as a decimal fraction
     Y = effective annual yield as a decimal fraction (after compounding)
     R = real annual interest rate (after inflation)
  RATS = real annual rate after taxes

     N = number of years
     Q = number of compounding periods per year
     U = number of remittances per year

     F = face value of discount paper
     P = price of discount paper

  YDAY = length of year in days (T-Bills=360)
  IDAY = length of investment in days

Appendix A

$I1 = I/Q$ = interest rate per period (substitute R/Q or RATS/Q if desired)
$N1 = N*Q$ = total number of compounding periods
$Q1 = Q/U$ = compounding periods per remittance period

T1 to T6 = temporary intermediate variables

$T1 = (1+I1)^{N1}$
$T2 = (1+I1)^{Q1}$

$T3 = (T1-1) / (T2-1)$
$T4 = (FV/PMT) * (T1-1)$

$T5 = (T1-1) / ((T2-1)*T1)$
$T6 = (PV/PMT) * (T1-1)$

Interest Rate Conversion Formulas:
$I = (365 * D) / (YDAY - (D*IDAY))$
$D = (YDAY * I) / (365 + (I*IDAY))$
$Y = ((1+I1)^Q)-1$
$R = (I * (1-INF)) - INF$
$RATS = ((I*(1-TAX)) * (1-INF)) - INF$

Lump Sum Formulas:
$PV = FV / T1$
$FV = PV * T1$
$N = (1/Q) * (LOG10(FV/PV) / LOG10(1+I1))$
$I = Q * (((FV/PV)^{(1/N1)}) - 1)$
Q = cannot be determined by formula

Future Value Annuities:
$FV = PMT * T3$
$PMT = FV / T3$
$N = (1/Q) * (LOG10(1+T4) / LOG10(1+I1))$
I = cannot be determined by formula
Q = cannot be determined by formula
U = cannot be determined by formula

Present Value Annuities:
$PV = PMT * T5$
$PMT = PV / T5$
$N = (-1/Q) * (LOG10(1-T6) / LOG10(1+I1))$
I = cannot be determined by formula

Q = cannot be determined by formula
U = cannot be determined by formula

Discount Securities:
   F = P / (1 - (D*(IDAY/YDAY))
   P = F * (1 - (D*(IDAY/YDAY))
   D = (1-(P/F)) * (YDAY/IDAY)

   I = (365 * D) / (YDAY - (D*IDAY))
   D = (YDAY * I) / (365 + (I*IDAY))

NOTE: Logarithms can be either common (LOG10) or natural (LOGe).

APPENDIX B

HISTORICAL INTEREST AND INFLATION RATES

This appendix contains the data used to draw figures 5.2 through 5.5. Those figures show the annual change in the Consumer Price Index from 1800 to 1982, the average annual interest rate offered by high-quality corporate bonds from 1857 to 1982, the real interest rate of those bonds after adjusting for inflation from 1857 to 1982, and the real rate of the bonds expressed as a 25-year moving average between 1881 (1857–1881) and 1982 (1958–1982).

The annual change in the Consumer Price Index was calculated from the index itself. For the years 1850 through 1970 this index is available in the U.S. Census Bureau's *Historical Statistics of the United States, Colonial Times to 1970, Bicentennial Edition, Part 1* (Series E-135, pages 210–211). The Consumer Price Index for later years can be found in the bureau's annual publication *Statistical Abstract of the United States*.

The interest rate data also come from *Historical Statistics of the United States*. The second volume of that work gives the average annual interest rates offered by corporate bonds rated Aaa by Moody's Investors Service from 1919 through 1970 (Series X-477, page 1003). It also gives the average annual rate paid by a select group of U.S. railroad bonds between 1857 and 1936 (Series X-476, page 1003). The data presented here uses the railroad bonds through 1930, when their rates were lower than those of the Moody's group, and Moody's group data thereafter, when railroad bonds were higher. For years after 1970, Moody's group data comes from the annual *Statistical Abstract*.

	Consumer Price Index 1967=100	Figure 5.2 CPI annual pct change	Figure 5.3 average corporate bond rate	Figure 5.4 real rate after inflation	Figure 5.5 real rate 25-year moving average
1982	289.1	6.13	13.79	6.81	1.65
1981	272.4	10.37	14.17	2.33	1.38
1980	246.8	13.52	11.94	-3.20	1.36
1979	217.4	11.26	9.63	-2.71	1.63
1978	195.4	7.66	8.73	.40	1.83
1977	181.5	6.45	8.02	1.05	1.91
1976	170.5	5.77	8.43	2.17	1.90
1975	161.2	9.14	8.83	-1.12	1.60
1974	147.7	10.97	8.57	-3.34	1.71
1973	133.1	6.23	7.44	.75	1.99
1972	125.3	3.30	7.21	3.67	1.76
1971	121.3	4.30	7.39	2.77	1.12
1970	116.3	5.92	8.04	1.64	.76
1969	109.8	5.37	7.03	1.28	.71
1968	104.2	4.20	6.18	1.72	.70
1967	100	2.88	5.51	2.47	.48
1966	97.2	2.86	5.13	2.13	.06
1965	94.5	1.72	4.49	2.69	-.12
1964	92.9	1.31	4.40	3.03	-.15
1963	91.7	1.21	4.26	2.99	-.10
1962	90.6	1.12	4.33	3.17	-.01
1961	89.6	1.01	4.35	3.29	-.16
1960	88.7	1.60	4.41	2.74	-.20
1959	87.3	.81	4.38	3.54	-.27
1958	86.6	2.73	3.79	.96	-.39
1957	84.3	3.56	3.89	.19	-.03
1956	81.4	1.50	3.36	1.81	.59
1955	80.2	-.37	3.06	3.44	1.07
1954	80.5	.50	2.90	2.39	1.22
1953	80.1	.75	3.20	2.42	1.30
1952	79.5	2.19	2.96	.71	1.44
1951	77.8	7.91	2.86	-5.27	1.66

(continued)

Appendix B

YEAR	Consumer Price Index 1967=100	Figure 5.2 CPI annual pct change	Figure 5.3 average corporate bond rate	Figure 5.4 real rate after inflation	Figure 5.5 real rate 25-year moving average
1950	72.1	.98	2.62	1.61	2.01
1949	71.4	-.97	2.66	3.66	2.03
1948	72.1	7.77	2.82	-5.17	2.07
1947	66.9	14.36	2.61	-12.12	2.40
1946	58.5	8.53	2.53	-6.22	3.34
1945	53.9	2.28	2.62	.28	4.27
1944	52.7	1.74	2.72	.94	3.82
1943	51.8	6.15	2.73	-3.59	3.37
1942	48.8	10.66	2.83	-8.13	2.98
1941	44.1	5.00	2.77	-2.37	2.77
1940	42	.96	2.84	1.85	2.73
1939	41.6	-1.42	3.01	4.47	2.80
1938	42.2	-1.86	3.19	5.11	2.74
1937	43	3.61	3.26	-.47	2.61
1936	41.5	.97	3.24	2.24	2.65
1935	41.1	2.49	3.60	1.02	2.73
1934	40.1	3.35	4.00	.52	2.70
1933	38.8	-5.13	4.49	9.86	2.84
1932	40.9	-10.31	5.01	15.83	2.77
1931	45.6	-8.80	4.58	13.78	2.15
1930	50	-2.53	4.41	7.06	1.76
1929	51.3	0.00	4.60	4.60	1.63
1928	51.3	-1.35	4.35	5.75	1.61
1927	52	-1.89	4.34	6.31	1.38
1926	53	.95	4.47	3.48	1.11
1925	52.5	2.54	4.73	2.07	1.13
1924	51.2	.20	4.84	4.63	1.20
1923	51.1	1.79	4.98	3.10	1.17
1922	50.2	-6.34	4.85	11.50	1.21
1921	53.6	-10.67	5.57	16.83	.91
1920	60	15.83	5.81	-10.94	.41
1919	51.8	14.86	5.29	-10.35	1.18
1918	45.1	17.45	5.23	-13.13	1.93
1917	38.4	17.43	4.79	-13.48	2.64

(continued)

Historical Interest and Inflation Rates **145**

YEAR	Consumer Price Index 1967=100	Figure 5.2 CPI annual pct change	Figure 5.3 average corporate bond rate	Figure 5.4 real rate after inflation	Figure 5.5 real rate 25-year moving average
1916	32.7	7.57	4.49	-3.42	3.36
1915	30.4	1.00	4.62	3.58	3.68
1914	30.1	1.35	4.44	3.03	3.72
1913	29.7	2.41	4.44	1.92	3.78
1912	29	3.57	4.23	.51	3.88
1911	28	0.00	4.19	4.19	4.05
1910	28	3.70	4.18	.32	4.06
1909	27	0.00	4.07	4.07	4.25
1908	27	-3.57	4.22	7.94	4.44
1907	28	3.70	4.27	.41	4.48
1906	27	0.00	4.00	4.00	4.67
1905	27	0.00	3.89	3.89	4.72
1904	27	0.00	3.98	3.98	4.64
1903	27	3.85	4.03	.03	4.86
1902	26	4.00	3.84	-.31	5.52
1901	25	0.00	3.83	3.83	5.79
1900	25	0.00	3.89	3.89	6.04
1899	25	0.00	3.85	3.85	6.29
1898	25	0.00	4.03	4.03	6.68
1897	25	0.00	4.11	4.11	6.83
1896	25	0.00	4.34	4.34	6.97
1895	25	-3.85	4.27	8.28	7.33
1894	26	-3.70	4.41	8.28	7.53
1893	27	0.00	4.65	4.65	7.53
1892	27	0.00	4.53	4.53	7.86
1891	27	0.00	4.71	4.71	8.19
1890	27	0.00	4.55	4.55	8.50
1889	27	0.00	4.43	4.43	8.72
1888	27	0.00	4.59	4.59	7.64
1887	27	0.00	4.65	4.65	6.72
1886	27	0.00	4.55	4.55	6.36
1885	27	0.00	4.89	4.89	6.53
1884	27	-3.57	5.15	8.91	6.68
1883	28	-3.45	5.23	8.86	6.51

(continued)

Appendix B

YEAR	Consumer Price Index 1967=100	Figure 5.2 CPI annual pct change	Figure 5.3 average corporate bond rate	Figure 5.4 real rate after inflation	Figure 5.5 real rate 25-year moving average
1882	29	0.00	5.24	5.24	6.84
1881	29	0.00	5.19	5.19	6.88
1880	29	3.57	5.60	1.83	
1879	28	-3.45	5.98	9.63	
1878	29	-9.38	6.45	16.43	
1877	32	0.00	6.62	6.62	
1876	32	-3.03	6.68	9.91	
1875	33	-2.94	7.06	10.21	
1874	34	-5.56	7.53	13.50	
1873	36	0.00	7.76	7.76	
1872	36	0.00	7.60	7.60	
1871	36	-5.26	7.78	13.45	
1870	38	-5.00	7.92	13.32	
1869	40	0.00	8.13	8.13	
1868	40	-4.76	7.80	12.93	
1867	42	-4.55	7.87	12.77	
1866	44	-4.35	7.95	12.64	
1865	46	-2.13	7.62	9.91	
1864	47	27.03	6.27	-22.45	
1863	37	23.33	6.34	-18.47	
1862	30	11.11	7.56	-4.39	
1861	27	0.00	8.88	8.88	
1860	27	0.00	8.59	8.59	
1859	27	3.85	8.91	4.72	
1858	26	-7.14	9.34	17.15	
1857	28	3.70	10.25	6.17	
1856	27	-3.57			
1855	28	3.70			
1854	27	8.00			
1853	25	0.00			
1852	25	0.00			
1851	25	0.00			
1850	25	0.00			
1849	25	-3.85			

(continued)

Historical Interest and Inflation Rates

YEAR	Consumer Price Index 1967=100	Figure 5.2 CPI annual pct change	Figure 5.3 average corporate bond rate	Figure 5.4 real rate after inflation	Figure 5.5 real rate 25-year moving average
1848	26	-7.14			
1847	28	3.70			
1846	27	-3.57			
1845	28	0.00			
1844	28	0.00			
1843	28	-3.45			
1842	29	-6.45			
1841	31	3.33			
1840	30	-6.25			
1839	32	0.00			
1838	32	-5.88			
1837	34	3.03			
1836	33	6.45			
1835	31	3.33			
1834	30	3.45			
1833	29	-3.33			
1832	30	-6.25			
1831	32	0.00			
1830	32	0.00			
1829	32	-3.03			
1828	33	-2.94			
1827	34	0.00			
1826	34	0.00			
1825	34	3.03			
1824	33	-8.33			
1823	36	-10.00			
1822	40	0.00			
1821	40	-4.76			
1820	42	-8.70			
1819	46	0.00			
1818	46	-4.17			
1817	48	-5.88			
1816	51	-7.27			
1815	55	-12.70			

(continued)

148 Appendix B

YEAR	Consumer Price Index 1967=100	Figure 5.2 CPI annual pct change	Figure 5.3 average corporate bond rate	Figure 5.4 real rate after inflation	Figure 5.5 real rate 25-year moving average
1814	63	8.62			
1813	58	13.73			
1812	51	2.00			
1811	50	6.38			
1810	47	0.00			
1809	47	-2.08			
1808	48	9.09			
1807	44	-6.38			
1806	47	4.44			
1805	45	0.00			
1804	45	0.00			
1803	45	4.65			
1802	43	-14.00			
1801	50	-1.96			
1800	51				
minimum	25	-14.00	2.53	-22.45	-.39
maximum	289.1	27.03	14.17	17.15	8.72

APPENDIX C

FURTHER READING

Here are a few books you may find helpful if you want to investigate interest rates further.

The Dow Jones-Irwin Guide to Interest by Lawrence R. Rosen (Homewood, Ill: Dow Jones-Irwin, 1974) is the book that first got me interested in the time value of money. Over half the book consists of interest-rate tables, which *Your Best Interest* makes obsolete, I hope. Another quarter of the book consists of graphs, however, which you may find useful in understanding the effect of time, compounding, and so on.

The Consumer's Guide to Banks by Gordon L. Weil (New York: Stein and Day, 1975) and *The Figure Finaglers* by Robert Reichard (New York: McGraw-Hill, 1974) are the two best books I've found on ways the true interest rate of a transaction can be raised or lowered at a professional's whim while the quoted interest rate is left untouched.

The Encyclopedia of Real Estate Formulas and Tables by Martin J. Miles (Englewood Cliffs: Prentice-Hall, 1978) is a terrific reference for standard interest-rate formulas. It goes way beyond what we've presented here, headed in the direction of real estate.

Money Market Calculations: Yields, Break-Evens, and Arbitrage by Marcia Stigum (Homewood, Ill: Dow Jones-Irwin, 1981) is another formula reference. It starts at a little higher level than the Miles book and heads off rapidly into such topics as "riding the yield curve." It includes a good introduction to the major money market instruments and how they work.

A History of Interest Rates by Sidney Homer (New Brunswick, N.J.: Rutgers University Press, 1977) is my favorite interest-rate book (present company excepted). This book starts with interest rates in prehistoric times, works its way through Greece and Rome, looks at the effect of usury laws in the Middle Ages, and continues to modern times. This book will give you an appreciation for credit and interest rates as a fundamental aspect of human society.

GLOSSARY

Add-On Interest a calculation method whereby a borrower is charged interest as if a loan will be repaid as a lump sum when, in fact, the borrower is to repay the loan in monthly installments. The true interest rate of the transaction is *much* higher than it appears to be. The method is forbidden in U.S. consumer loans by the Truth-in-Lending law.

Adjustable-Rate Mortgage a mortgage that has interest rates that change periodically according to a predetermined formula.

Adventures a good thing to spend your money on. Unfortunately, such expenses don't increase the kind of net worth accountants keep track of. See *Taj Mahal* for more information.

Algorithm a programming formula or recipe.

Amortization the process of paying off a mortgage. As a mortgage is amortized, the borrower's equity increases.

Amortization Table a table showing how much of each remittance pays interest and how much redeems principal.

Annuity (uh-NEW-ity) a series, or stream, of remittances—payments or deposits. In this book we usually assume that the remittances are equal, but not everyone does that.

APR Annual Percentage Rate. This is the formal name for the "true interest rate."

Assets primarily, the things you own that have an economic life; but can also include investments and cash on hand.

Assumption the process whereby a home buyer accepts responsibility for a seller's mortgage. There is no cheaper way to obtain large amounts of money than by assuming a low-interest mortgage.

Balloon Payment a larger than normal payment in a series of remittances. Balloon payments usually, but not necessarily, occur at the end of the series.

Buy-Down an advance payment made in return for a lower apparent interest rate on a loan or mortgage. The true interest rate of the transaction rarely changes much, since the advance payment effectively lowers the present value of the transaction. However, if the borrower pays the loan or mortgage off early, the true interest rate of the transaction will jump upward.

Capital Expenses transactions that buy items that have an economic life. Funds spent on a car or a printing press would be captial expenses; funds spent on gasoline or paper would not.

Cash Flow the difference bewteen an investment's income and expenses. The expenses used in calculating cash flow include both operating expenses and capital expenses and, therefore, do not include depreciation expenses.

Certificate of Deposit interest-bearing paper issued by a bank or other financial institution.

Collateral an asset that has been pledged to someone as security for a loan. If the loan is not repaid, the lender can take possession of the collateral.

Compound Interest interest earned on both the principal and retained interest of an investment. When you withdraw the interest you have earned from an investment, the investment is earning simple interest. When you leave the interest you have earned on deposit to earn its own interest, the investment is earning compound interest.

Compounding Period the amount of time that passes before the amount of interest earned by an investment is calculated and added to the investment. Typical compounding periods are daily, monthly, quarterly, semiannually, and annually.

Coupon/Coupons relating to interest-bearing notes or bonds. The notes or bonds themselves are sometimes called "coupons"; the interest rate they earn is called the "coupon rate." Some bonds come with coupons attached that must be torn off by the holder and sent to the issuer to collect interest.

Crediting/Crediting Period the process of actually placing interest you have earned in your account. "Daily compounding" implies daily crediting, but few financial institutions actually credit more often than monthly.

Decimal Fraction a whole percentage divided by 100. For example, 10 per cent is 10/100 or .10 when expressed as a decimal fraction.

Depreciation the process whereby the value of an asset decreases because of wear and tear. Depreciation is an operating expense. Capital expenses turn into operating expenses by means of depreciation.

Discount The word "discount" has three separate and distinct meanings in the world of interest rates. First, there's the discount method of calculating interest. In this method the percentage is applied to the amount that will be paid back (future value) rather than to the amount borrowed (present value). A discount interest rate is always lower than the true interest rate. Secondly, there's the discount rate of a cash flow. This is the true interest rate used to determine the present value of a cash flow in return-on-investment analysis. Third, and least important to individuals, there's the discount rate the Federal Reserve charges banks for loans.

Glossary

Effective Annual Yield the interest rate you would have to earn on a one-year simple-interest investment to obtain as much actual interest as you'd get at a lower, compounded rate.

Equity the portion of an asset that has been paid for. If you borrow $90,000 to buy a $100,000 home, your equity in the home is 10 per cent.

Escrow Account funds collected by a lender as part of your monthly mortgage payment to cover property taxes and homeowner's insurance. Payments into an escrow account are over and above the monthly payments determined by interest-rate formulas.

Estate what you leave behind when you die; the whole of your possessions, including all assets and all debts.

Exact Time a method of calculating time for interest-rate transactions in which the exact number of calendar days is used. A year has 365 days in exact time, except during leap year, when it has 366.

Future Value the value of a financial tranaction at some point in the future, as distinct from the present moment.

Future Value Annuity a stream of remittances that has a zero present value and a lump-sum future value. A typical example is an IRA account.

Goliah a mathematical process whereby an answer to a problem is determined by constructing a complete representation of the problem with a spreadsheet program. This is distinct from solving the problem with summary formulas. The word "goliah" is a combination of the words golem, Goliath, and formula. It connotes solving a puzzle by creating a giant, detailed impersonation, forcing it to life with brute mathematical strength, and watching it attack the great dark void of ignorance.

Interest a fee for the use of money.

Iteration the process of repeating a mathematical calculation over and over with different input variables until a predetermined output variable results.

Liabilities debts; what you owe. Everything you have borrowed from someone else is a liability.

Marginal Tax Rate see "Tax Bracket."

Negative Amortization a situation that can occur with adjustable-rate mortgages that cap the monthly payment instead of the interest rate. If interest rates go high enough, the monthly payment won't cover interest charges. In this eventuality, excess interest is added to the mortgage's balance. At the end of the year you owe *more* than you did at the beginning.

Net Worth the extent to which your life income has exceeded your life expenses. Net worth is calculated by subtracting all your liabilities from all your assets.

Offsetting Balance a requirement that part of a loan must be left on deposit at the lending institution. The requirement raises the true interest rate of the loan.

Operating Expenses expenses for items that are consumed, such as electricity or linefeeds. Funds spent on gasoline or paper would be operating expenses; funds spent on cars or printing presses would not.

Ordinary Time a method of calculating time for interest-rate transactions in which all months are assumed to have 30 days and a year 360 days.

Origination Fees fees paid in order to obtain a loan or mortgage. These fees raise the true interest rate of the transaction.

Points fees paid to a lender to obtain a loan or mortgage. One point is equivalent to 1 per cent of the face value of the transaction. Points raise the true interest rate of the transaction.

Prepayment Penalty a penalty, agreed upon by a lender and a borrower at the time of an initial transaction, that is imposed on the borrower if the borrower pays off the loan or mortgage early.

Present Value the value of a financial transaction at the present moment, as distinct from some future moment.

Present Value Annuity a stream of remittances that has a zero future value and a lump-sum present value. A typical example is a home mortgage.

Principal the main body of an investment; distinct from interest, which is earned by principal. If you invest $1,000 in a money market fund, the $1,000 is your principal.

Real Interest Rate the rate of interest earned after adjusting for inflation.

Refinancing getting a new low-interest loan and using the proceeds to pay off an old high-interest loan. Borrowers have incentive to do this when interest rates fall.

Remittance a payment or a deposit. As used in this book, remittances usually occur according to a predetermined, periodic schedule. Time-value formulas assume all remittances are made at the end of each period.

Simple Interest interest earned only on the principal of an investment. When you withdraw the interest you have earned from an investment, the investment is earning simple interest. When you leave the interest you have earned on deposit to earn its own interest, the investment is earning compound interest.

Taj Mahal a magnificent white marble monument built by an Indian raja, or king, in honor of his wife, Mumtaz Mahal, who died at the age of 39 after giving birth to her fourteenth child. The Taj was built adjacent to the Jumna River in the 1600s near the city of Agra. The king, Shah Jahan, planned to build a black-marble duplicate of the Taj across the river in commemoration of himself, but his son Aurangzeb imprisoned him for self-indulgence. As you make your final approach to the Taj Mahal, you will prepare yourself for disappointment. But from your first glimpse through the great gate in the surrounding sandstone wall, the Taj will fill you with pleasure. During the Indo-Pak War of 1971, the Taj Mahal was reportedly covered with burlap bags to prevent Pakistani pilots from using it as a reference point during nighttime bombing runs. The war ended, thank God, when both sides ran out of gas. See *Adventures*.

Tax Bracket that which determines the percentage of tax paid on the last dollar earned by an individual. Because the percentage of tax paid increases as income increases, your tax bracket depends on your income. Use IRS Schedule X,Y,Z to determine your tax bracket.

Teaser Rate a deceptively low interest rate charged during the first calculation period of an adjustable-rate mortgage. A true rate for the first period, calculated using both the teaser rate and the origination fee, will show how deceptive the teaser rate is.

Template a model worksheet for a spreadsheet program such as VisiCalc.

Term Insurance a type of life insurance that pays off if you die and offers nothing more. Term insurance is considerably cheaper than other types of life insurance and is well-suited for parents of small children.

Time Value Because money can earn interest, it has time value. A dollar in hand today is worth more than a dollar in hand next month because of the interest it can earn in the meantime.

Treasury Bills a security issued by the U.S. Treasury with a maturity of one year or less. T-bills are issued at a discount from face value. T-bills are quoted with discount rates; the true rate paid by a T-bill is higher than it appears.

Treasury Bond an interest-bearing security issued by the U.S. Treasury, with a maturity of ten years or more. Interest is paid to the holder based on the bond's coupon. The holder may also have a capital gain or loss if the bond is purchased after issue or sold before redemption.

Treasury Note the same thing as a Treasury bond except that the maturity is shorter—anywhere from one to ten years.

Truth-in-Lending a body of government regulations that force lenders to disclose to consumers the true interest rate (APR) they are charging, as well as other details of a loan.

Wealth in a strict accounting sense, the extent to which your life income has exceeded your life expenses. Some things not usually counted as wealth, however, such as adventures and education, clearly have a permanent value—you may want to include them in your own accounting of wealth.

INDEX

@COUNT 16, 18
@NPV 84–85, 135

add-on interest 107–108, 151
adjustable–rate mortgages
   117–123, 133, 151
adventures 90, 151
algorithm 151 (see formulas)
amortization 43, 53, 151
   negative 153
   table 43, 53–54, 151
annuity 38–44, 56, 151
answer window 15, 19
APR 151
assets 57–59, 64, 89–90, 151
assumption 115–117, 151
asterisk 5

balance 53, 68
   methods for calculating 53, 129
balloon payment 79–81, 151
base 7
BASIC 5, 10, 65
bonds 95, 101, 133–136 (also see savings bonds, treasury bonds)

business loans 52, 60, 111–113
buy-downs 112–113, 114–115, 152

calculation order 13, 53, 65
calculation section 18
capital expenses 57, 81, 152
caps 120–121
cash
   cash flow 82, 85, 152
   free cash offer 173
   cash value 91
caret 6
capital gain 135
certificates of deposit 23–24, 60, 131, 132, 152
collateral 60, 152
commitment period 60–61
compound growth 35–36
compound interest 24–25, 29, 152
   magic of 25
   loses charm 97
compounding frequency/period 28–29, 33, 44, 67–71, 78–79, 128, 152
Consumer Price Index 98, 101, 142–148

158 Index

cosigning 62
coupon 134, 152
credit cards 109–110
credit life insurance 110
crediting/crediting period 128, 152

debts (see liabilities)
decimal fractions 8, 17, 68, 152
defaulting 136
deflation 98
demand accounts 61, 128–131
depreciation 57, 64, 152
discount 152
    cash flow 82–84, 107
    interest 28, 62, 106–107, 132–133
    rate 107
ducks 21

economic life 57
education 90
effective annual yield 28–29, 30, 130, 153
errors
    error checking 16
    rounding error 35
equity 59, 64, 153
escrow account 122, 153
estate 89–90, 153
exact time 33, 129–130, 153
expenses 57, 64
    capital 57, 152
    operating 57, 153
exponents 6

financial tables 4–5, 35, 44
formulas (summary 139–141)
    compound growth 25
    future value of lump sums 30
    future value of a series of remittances 45–46
    per cent 10
    per cent change 10
    present value of lump sums 30
    present value of a series of remittances 50
frequency of compounding (see compounding frequency)
future value 26–27, 29, 153
future value annuity 40–42, 45–49, 153

gifts 130
gold 101, 126
goliah 56, 153
gross national product 71–72
growth rates 35–37

hold on deposits 130
home mortgages (see mortgages)

income 57, 64
income tax (see taxes)
inflation 96–104, 126
    historical levels 142–148
insurance (see life insurance)
interest 3, 23–24, 153
    interest-bearing accounts 127–131
    interest-bearing paper 131–136
    formula summary 139–141
    historical rate levels 142–148
    other books about 149–150
    rates 7
    real interest rates 97–104
internal rate of return 84–85
IRA (Individual Retirement Account) 48, 95
iteration 45, 49, 153

liabilities 59–60, 64, 89–90, 153
life insurance 49, 90–92, 110, 126, 155

lottery 77–78
lump sums 23–37, 41

marginal tax rate 92–93, 98, 154
meaning of life 126
money market funds 62–63
money trees 3–4, 24, 28
mortgages 51, 73–76, 111–123
   adjustable rate mortgages 117–123, 133
   calculating mortgage balance 53
   escrow accounts 122
   graduated payment mortgages 121
   reverse annuity mortgages 40
   value of low-interest mortgages 116–117

negative amortization 121, 153
net present value 84–85
net worth 64, 89–90, 153

offsetting balance 112, 153
operating expenses 57, 153
ordinary time 33, 129–130, 132–133, 153
origination fees 111–112, 113, 114–115, 119, 154

parentheses 6
part 7
payback period 81
percentage points 9
percentages 7–9, 13–20
per cent change 8–9, 20–21
points 114, 154
precision 35
prepayment penalty 114–115, 154
present value 26–27, 29, 154
present value annuity 39, 42–44, 50–53, 154

prime rate 62
principal 24, 29, 127–129, 154
   methods for calculating 129

question window 14–16

real estate 101, 136
real interest rate 97–104, 154
recalculation 13, 20, 65
refinancing 117, 154
reciprocal 6
regulation Z 106
remittance 38, 44, 69, 78–79, 154
   at end of period 41, 48–49
   unequal 56
return on investment analysis 59, 81–85
reverse annuity mortgage 40
risk 61–62
rock-chalk 21
root 6
rounding error 35

salary 21, 51
savings bonds 132
secured loans 62
share 19
simple interest 23–24, 29, 43, 154
slash 6
spreadsheet 5, 11, 56
   @COUNT 16, 18
   column width 13, 65
   calculation order 13, 65
   @NPV 84–85, 135
   recalculation 13, 20, 65
   wrap-around technique 73–74
stocks 101, 136
stock option 32

tables, financial 4–5, 35, 44
Taj Mahal 90, 154

taxes 92–96
  average tax rate 92–93, 98
  deductibility of interest 96
  marginal tax rate 92–93, 98, 154
  Rate Schedule X,Y,Z 93–94
  tax bracket 92–93, 154
  tax consequences of buy–downs 113
  tax-free investments 93–95
  tax-sheltered investments 95
teaser rate 118–120, 154
templates 12, 155
  future value of a series of remittances 46–47
  goliah 65–69
  percentages 14–19
  per cent change 20–21
  present value of a series of remittances 50–51
  standard template 13–19
  time value of a lump sum 30–31
term insurance (see life insurance)
test data
  future value of a series of remittances 48–49
  growth rates 36
  lump sums 32–35
  percentages 19–20
  per cent change 21
  present value of a series of remittances 51–52
time value 4, 23, 28, 81, 155
time period calculations 33, 129–130, 132–133
transaction size 61
transformation section 17
traveler's checks 127
treasury bills 62, 107, 118, 131–133, 155
treasury bonds 133–136, 155
treasury notes 133–136, 155
trusts 32
truth-in-lending 106, 110, 111, 125, 155

unsecured loans 62

VisiCalc 5, 12

wars 98
wealth 57, 64, 89–90, 155
worksheets (see templates)
wrap-around problem solving 73–74

yield of bonds 135–136

zero-coupon bonds 136